Order of the Arrow Handbook

Boy Scouts of America

My Brother:

As you have been chosen to serve among your peers, this handbook will act as your guide and inspiration on your pathway of servant leadership. The journey is long and your burden heavy, but with the help of our brothers you will succeed as those who have gone before you. Keep this guidebook close at hand, and together we will discover the limitless possibilities of the Order of the Arrow.

Yours in brotherhood,

Nicholas G. Dannemiller
National Chief
Inducted May 2007

Taylor L. Bobrow
National Vice Chief
Inducted May 2008

Ray Capp
National Chairman
Inducted July 1965

Clyde M. Mayer
Director
Inducted June 1975

34996
ISBN 978-0-8395-4996-3
©2009 Boy Scouts of America

Contents

Order of the Arrow
Personal Record

Name: _____

Street: _____

City, State: _____

Ordeal Membership

Calling Out: Date: _____

     Location: _____

Ceremony: Date: _____

     Location: _____

Lodge: _____

Brotherhood Membership

Ceremony: Date: _____

     Location: _____

Lodge: _____

Vigil Honor

Calling Out: Date: _____

     Location: _____

Ceremony: Date: _____

     Location: _____

Vigil Honor Indian Name:

English Translation:

Lodge: _____

Offices Held:

Section and National Events Attended:

Foreword

For those readers who are new Arrowmen, welcome! This edition of the *Order of the Arrow Handbook* has been written especially for you, for you are the future of the Order.

To veteran members of the Order, you will find this edition helpful in many ways. While some sections and words will seem familiar, take note that much of what is contained between the covers of this handbook is important to all Arrowmen.

This handbook brings together the basic knowledge that all members will want to know. In addition, many topics have been expanded for clarity and emphasis.

For more information on the current policies concerning the Order of the Arrow lodge, refer to the *Order of the Arrow Guide for Officers and Advisers,* which is available for download and printing at the Order's official website: http://www.oa-bsa.org.

Scouting's National Honor Society

Membership Requirements

- Be a registered member of the Boy Scouts of America.

- After registration with a troop or team, have experienced 15 days and nights of Boy Scout camping during the two-year period prior to election. The 15 days and nights must include one, but no more than one, long-term camp consisting of six consecutive days and five nights of resident camping, approved and under the auspices and standards of the BSA. The balance of the camping must be overnight, weekend, or other short-term camps.

- Youth must be under the age of 21, hold the BSA First Class rank or higher, and following approval by the Scoutmaster or Varsity Coach, be elected by the youth members of their troop or team. Adults may be selected following nomination to the lodge adult selection committee.

Purpose and Principles

You may recall that Meteu recounted the legend of the Lenni Lenape Indians during the final part of the Ordeal Ceremony. Among the things he said: "In a great and honored Order, into which can be admitted only those who unselfishly desire to serve others, there must be a lofty purpose. You were selected for membership in the Order because your fellow Scouts saw your sincerity and acceptance of the high ideals of the Scout Oath and Law."

As a member of the Order of the Arrow, you are a member of Scouting's National Honor Society. You must fulfill the trust and confidence bestowed upon you by your fellow Scouts with this mighty purpose: The essence of our existence is that we must be those campers—Boy Scouts, Varsity Scouts, and Scouters—who best exemplify the Scout Oath and Law in our daily lives and by such conduct cause others to emulate our actions. We who bear the Obligation of the Order of the Arrow, mindful of our high tradition, ponder that which is our purpose, and do pledge ourselves to cheerful service.

MISSION STATEMENT

The mission of the Order of the Arrow is to fulfill its purpose as an integral part of the Boy Scouts of America through positive youth leadership under the guidance of selected capable adults.

For further interpretation and explanation, see page 87.

PURPOSE OF THE ORDER

As Scouting's National Honor Society, our purpose is to:

- *Recognize those who best exemplify the Scout Oath and Law in their daily lives and through that recognition cause others to conduct themselves in a way that warrants similar recognition.*

- *Promote camping, responsible outdoor adventure, and environmental stewartship as essential components of every Scout's experience, in the unit, year-round, and in summer camp.*

- *Develop leaders with the willingness, character, spirit, and ability to advance the activities of their units, our Brotherhood, Scouting, and ultimately our nation.*

- *Crystallize the Scout habit of helpfulness into a life purpose of leadership in cheerful service to others.*

For further interpretation and explanation, see page 89.

PRINCIPLES OF THE ORDER

The Order of the Arrow was founded upon the principles of brotherhood, cheerfulness, and service. These principles form the foundation for the Obligation of the Order. In pledging this Obligation, you promise, on your honor, "to be unselfish in service and devotion to the welfare of others." This is not an easy pledge to fulfill, for there are few who live a life of cheerful service in our world. For some, the Order will be like a supernova, shining brilliantly for a brief time and soon crumbling to ashes. For others, the Order will kindle a flame of brotherhood, brighter than a thousand suns, lasting throughout eternity.

During your candidacy, you have impressed upon those fellow members who have lived closest to you the sincerity of your purpose to live in accordance with the high ideals of the Scout Oath. The judgment of your fellows can hardly have been mistaken.

You were inducted into the Order of the Arrow "not so much for what you have done, but for what you are expected to do." Now the time to judge has come. You have entered our Brotherhood. The distinctive pocket emblem and sash are yours. Now you are to face another test, one administered and graded solely by yourself. Will you embrace the traditions and obligations of our Order?

Your election into our Order was indeed unique. There is no other organization in which members are elected by both members and nonmembers.

Any organization that inducts only from within is prone to lose touch with society, but your election was based on the standards set by your fellow Scouts. Thus the Order, grounded in outdoor camping, will continue to be relevant to today's society.

CAMPING AND THE ORDER

Camping is a method of Scouting, but camping is not Scouting's purpose. Scouting aims to build character, citizenship, and fitness. When Scouts go camping, this growth just seems to follow. Patrol and troop camping are models and a testing ground for life in society. In a small group, each member is dependent on the others. Each learns to accept responsibility and to exercise good judgment. Even a stubborn or selfish person finds himself interacting with others in helpful and supportive ways. Scouts who camp will sooner or later come face to face with practical applications of the Scout Oath and Law. Cheerfulness, trustworthiness, courtesy, helpfulness, and all the central virtues of Scouting are necessary in camp and in society. Life in the open is a natural teacher of these essential survival skills. Thus, we promote camping, and camping becomes more effective in achieving the aims of Scouting.

The principles of Scouting are central to any kind of successful camping. The Order of the Arrow arose in a Scout camp, and it keeps camping promotion as a major service. Arrowmen encourage Scouts to go camping. In camp we maintain the best traditions and the highest spirit.

FUTURE OF THE ORDER

As we move further into the next century of service, the vision for the Order of the Arrow is to further our recognition as Scouting's National Honor Society and as an integral part of every local council. Our service, activities, adventures, and training for youth and adults serve as models of quality leadership development and programming that enrich, support, and help extend Scouting to America's youth.

The Order of the Arrow intends to dramatically increase its level of service to local councils and to the national organization. We intend to do more—much more—to help the Boy Scouts of America fulfill its mission to serve our nation's youth. In the years ahead we will expand our reach beyond camping to include greater focus on leadership development, membership extension, adventurous programming, and broader service to Scouting and the community.

As a member of the Order, you are essential to the success of the Order of the Arrow's future and the future of Scouting. Now is the time for you to commit yourself to our vision of the future, our strategy for getting there, and our mutual success.

Order of the Arrow Obligation

*I do hereby promise, on my honor as a Scout,
that I will always and faithfully observe and
preserve the traditions of the Order of the Arrow,
Wimachtendienk, Wingolauchsik, Witahemui.*

*I will always regard the ties of brotherhood
in the Order of the Arrow as lasting, and will
seek to preserve a cheerful spirit, even
in the midst of irksome tasks and weighty
responsibilities, and will endeavor, so far as
in my power lies, to be unselfish in service
and devotion to the welfare of others.*

(Sign your name.)

THE OBLIGATION

Although our many service projects are valuable to Scouting, the main benefit
is less obvious. The Order's primary concern is the individual, and the Order's
function is to spread the spirit of brotherhood and cheerful service. You do
the work of the Order in your home, your troop or team, and your school,
as you keep the fire of the Scout Oath alive in words and deeds. More than
anything else, your own example of cheerful service to others accomplishes
the Order's aim.

"Wimachtendienk, Wingolauchsik, Witahemui" means "the brotherhood
of cheerful service" or "brotherhood, cheerfulness, and service," the three
principles of the Order. Thus the second sentence of the Obligation is an explanation of the first.

The Obligation of the Order is one way we remind ourselves of our special duties. Memorize it just as you did the Scout Oath and Law. Remember the three principles of the Order, and you will easily learn it.

Your actions in living the Obligation as a member of your troop or team fulfill the primary goals of the Order. As you read, you will see how you can promote camping and camping traditions in your troop or team, how you can help your fellow Scouts, and how you can participate in the activities of the Order. But remember the main work of the Order is done by you, usually alone and without praise or reward. "He alone is worthy to wear the Arrow who will continue faithfully to serve his fellow man."

When Dr. E. Urner Goodman and his Treasure Island camp staff started the Order in 1915, they realized that the Scouts who were to be chosen to set the example in their troops would need further encouragement and inspiration if they were to fulfill their role in Scouting. They devised the Ordeal to give the new Arrowmen this inspiration in the form of an experience involving the ideals they were to follow:

- Eat you nothing but the scant food you'll be given. Learn by fasting, sacrifice, and self-denial to subordinate personal desires to the spirit's higher purpose.

- Your directions are the whispers, urgings, promptings, deep within your hearts and spirits. Therefore, till you take the Obligation, strictly keep a pledge of silence.

- Spend the day in arduous labor, working gladly, not begrudging, seek to serve, and thus be faithful to the high ideals and purpose of the Order of the Arrow.

- All your strength will be required when you face the isolation that a leader often faces. So tonight beneath the heavens sleep alone upon your groundsheet.

The Ordeal has a different meaning to each candidate who completes it. The physical tests are deeply significant. It is a time of deep searching and high resolve; a unique opportunity to experience all the richness and warmth of brotherhood. Candidates need this experience not only for their own benefit, but also because their Obligation will require unusual devotion to the work of bringing this spirit to their own Scout troop or team.

The "induction sequence" is at the heart of the Order. The purpose of the induction is to encourage and inspire Arrowmen in the ideals of the Order and Scouting. It is by this method that we also pass along our traditions.

Your induction began with your election by your fellow Scouts. They selected you for your dedication to the ideals of Scouting. They look to you for leadership.

The term "induction sequence" is used in recognition of the fact that events in our induction must necessarily occur in a particular order, not at random. Following your election, you were called out. Then came your Ordeal, which began with the pre-Ordeal ceremony before an unlit fire, and ended with the Ordeal ceremony before a blazing campfire where you accepted the Obligation and received your Ordeal sash.

The next step in your induction is yours to carry out. Think about what you learned at your Ordeal and start applying it to your daily life. When you have made the principles of the Order part of your life, you are ready to complete your induction by "sealing your membership" in the Order of the Arrow through Brotherhood membership.

The purpose of Scouting is to build character, citizenship, and fitness. Camping is one of the most important ways these attributes are learned in the Scouting program. The Order of the Arrow arose in a camping situation, and has kept camping promotion as a major emphasis in order to further the aims of Scouting.

The American Indian cultures foster a love of the outdoors and nature. They use ceremonies to bind themselves together; to remind themselves of their obligations to themselves and each other. They set aside times for meditation, silence, isolation, fasting, and special duties to the tribe. The Order of the Arrow helps preserve this cultural perspective in camping promotion and induction. While we often celebrate our interest in American Indian culture with authentic dances and crafts, you do not need Indian attire, or an interest or ability in Indian lore or crafts to be a good Arrowman. Indian lore unto itself is colorful and interesting, but it is the inner strengths and fortitude of the American Indians that we seek to emphasize. To this end, the Order of the Arrow does more than place an emphasis on camping; it encourages the sort of Scout activity that fosters character development, citizenship training, and physical fitness.

The Ordeal is an adventure of the spirit; a time of deep searching and high resolve; a unique opportunity to experience all of the richness and warmth of brotherhood.

ORDER OF THE ARROW OFFICIAL SONG

Words by E. Urner Goodman

Music by Alexi Lvov,
"National Anthem of Tsarist Russia 1833–1917,"
as modified by E. Urner Goodman

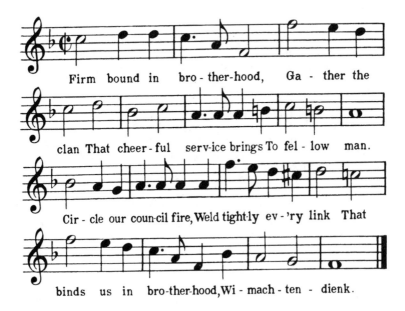

Order of the Arrow events and meetings are closed by forming a fellowship circle, joining hands right over left, and singing the official song.

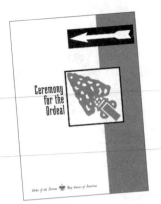

Obtain a copy of *Ceremony for the Ordeal* to learn more about the significance of the physical tests and each part of the Ordeal. This publication is a resource of information on a variety of topics, including the ceremony and ceremonial grounds setup, the Legend in prose, and a pronunciation guide. The entire ceremony is also included.

The Ten Induction Principles outline the basic philosophy and spirit behind the Ordeal induction. These points help to ensure the impressive nature of our ceremonies and remind us of the process and procedure to follow.

THE TEN INDUCTION PRINCIPLES

Principle One — Purpose: The purpose of the induction is to encourage and inspire each candidate to develop firm individual dedication to the ideals of brotherhood and cheerful service.

Principle Two — Eligibility: The right to earn Ordeal and Brotherhood membership is given only by the Scouts of a candidate's home unit during an authorized Order of the Arrow unit election. Only the candidate can overrule their decision.

Principle Three — Candidate's Compliance: The candidate has the continuous choice of meeting the tests of the Ordeal to the best of his or her ability or of withdrawing.

Principle Four — Members' Compliance: All members participating in the induction must respect and comply with the tests of the Ordeal, to the extent allowed by their responsibilities.

Principle Five — Discretion: In cases where strict application of the tests and requirements of the induction is not possible, the lodge may choose an alternative that will best preserve the spirit of the induction and the quality of the candidate's experience.

Principle Six — Importance of the Individual: All actions and procedures must recognize the worth, dignity, and separate identity of the individual and present or potential ability to self-govern.

Principle Seven — Generosity: The attitude of members toward the candidate must be one of acceptance, respect, understanding, sincerity, friendly encouragement, support, and trust.

Principle Eight — Focus: Everything in the lodge-created environment must direct the candidate to the central meaning of the induction, without distraction.

Principle Nine — Symbolic Progression: No symbol or symbolic procedure should be mentioned or used unless and until it is called for in the authorized ceremonies.

Principle Ten — Active Membership: Lodge policy must recognize that if a member understands the Obligation of the Order and is striving to fulfill it, he is an active member, and this dedication in itself accomplishes the major service of the lodge.

HISTORY

The Order of the Arrow was founded to serve a useful purpose: to cause the Scout Oath and Law to spring into action in all parts of the nation. To this day, we are dedicated to this high purpose.

The Order is a thing of the individual rather than a thing of the masses. The principles of brotherhood, cheerfulness, and service spring to life in each of us. What each Arrowman does counts toward the success we have as an organization.

The Order is a thing of the outdoors. It was born in an island wilderness. It needs and is nurtured by the sun and the rain, the mountains and the plains, the woods, the waters, and the starlit sky.

From life in the wilds comes a precious ingredient that our country, and any country, needs to survive — self-reliance, making us strong in times of stress. One of the Order's greatest achievements is, and will continue to be, the strengthening of the Scouting movement as an outdoor experience.

Dr. E. Urner Goodman, founder of the Order of the Arrow, once said:

"The Order is a thing of the spirit rather than of mechanics. Organization, operational procedures, and all that go with them are necessary in any large and growing movement, but they are not what counts in the end. The things of the spirit are what count:

Brotherhood — in a day when there is too much hatred at home and abroad

Cheerfulness — in a day when the pessimists have the floor and cynics are popular

Service — in a day when millions are interested in getting or grasping, rather than giving"

The Order's role includes service to Scouting on a national, regional, and sectional level, but it is our own council that needs us most. The Order is not an end unto itself, but is for a higher purpose.

The Order of the Arrow was founded during the summer of 1915 at Treasure Island, the Philadelphia Council Scout camp. Treasure Island was part of the original land grant given to William Penn by King Charles II of England. The camp was located on a 50-acre wooded island in the Delaware River between New Jersey and Pennsylvania, 30 miles upriver from Trenton and 3 miles from Point Pleasant. Historical records show that it was an early camping ground of the Lenni Lenape or Delaware Indians.

Dr. E. Urner Goodman,
founder of the
Order of the Arrow

In May 1915, a young man named E. Urner Goodman was selected to serve as summer camp director of Treasure Island. Another young man, Carroll A. Edson, was appointed assistant director in charge of the commissary. Both men were 24 years old.

Goodman had been a Scoutmaster in Philadelphia and had considerable experience in Scouting and camping. Edson was a graduate of Dartmouth College and had also been in Scouting for several years. After their appointments were announced, they spent many hours together planning their summer camping season, and both did considerable reading and research to better prepare themselves for their new responsibilities.

Among the books Goodman read, several were about camping. One of these that impressed him the most, a book dealing with summer camp operation, contained a description of a camp society that had been organized at a camp to perpetuate its traditions and ideals from season to season. Goodman and Edson agreed that they wanted to establish a similar society at their camp. They wanted some definite form of recognition for those Scouts in their camp who best exemplified the spirit of the Scout Oath and Law in their daily lives. Since the Delaware Valley was rich in Indian tradition, and the island had been used in early times as an Indian camping ground, it seemed only natural to base this honor society on the legend and traditions of the Delaware Indians.

Shortly after it had been announced that he was selected to serve as assistant camp director, Carroll Edson went home for a weekend visit. During that visit, he attended a meeting where Ernest Thompson Seton, Chief Scout of the Boy Scouts of America, was speaking. Seton described how, when organizing an earlier youth movement called the Woodcraft Indians, he had much success by utilizing American Indian ceremonies at camp. This crystallized Goodman and Edson's idea of using the lore and legends of the Delaware Indians in their new brotherhood.

As a result, they prepared a simple yet effective ceremony that, in turn, led to the organization of what was later to become known as the Order of the Arrow. It was agreed from the beginning that the procedures and programs of the organization were to be based on the ideals of democracy. In their initial decisions, Goodman and Edson reflected those ideals by planning to elect members into the first lodge from the troops encamped at Treasure Island.

Carroll A. Edson

Thus, from the beginning, a unique custom was established in that members were elected by non-members. There has been no change in this since that time. The original name, Wimachtendienk, Wingolauchsik, Witahemui, was suggested by Horace W. Ralston, a Philadelphia Scouter. Ralston and Horace P. Kern had done most of the research on the Delaware Indians.

Soon after camp opened, Goodman explored the island to find the most appropriate setting for the ceremonial ground. He selected a site in the south woods of the island, far removed from the ordinary activities of camp, and Edson agreed that it would be an ideal spot. It was considerably off the beaten path, and because of its location was an excellent site.

The site chosen was a natural amphitheater formed by a ravine in dense woods. There was a clearing with sloping ground on one side, which lent itself well to spectator seating. The site was cleared of brush and a path cut through thick underbrush from the camp to the site.

Friday, July 16, 1915, dawned bright and clear on Treasure Island. In addition to the heavy heat that often hangs over the valley of the Delaware, there was something else in the air. It was an almost indescribable feeling of expectancy and mystery. By sundown the air was charged with a tense excitement. Those who were present always remembered the first induction into what is now known as the Order of the Arrow.

As darkness fell, the campers were lined up in single file by Harry Yoder, who acted as guide and guardian of the trail. In total silence the campers followed the guide by a roundabout route through the woods to the site of the council fire. The path led down a small ravine across which lay an old fallen tree. The boys were unaware that they were approaching the council fire until suddenly it was revealed. It was built in a triangular shape. Behind it, in long black robes, stood the founder of the Order of the Arrow—E. Urner Goodman, Chief of the Fire, and his assistant, Carroll A. Edson, Vice Chief of the Fire. The Chief of the Fire wore on his robe a turtle superimposed upon a triangle, denoting leadership, and the Vice Chief of the Fire, then called Sachem, wore a turtle without the triangle. (The turtle is the totem of the Unami Lodge.)

The early ceremony was quite different from what developed later. The ceremony presented three lessons:

1. The candidate attempted to encircle a large tree, individually, with outstretched arms. Having failed, he then was joined by several of the brothers who together had no difficulty encircling the large tree, thus teaching Brotherhood.

2. The candidate was directed to endeavor to scale a steep bank at the edge of the council ring. Failing in this, he again was assisted by the brothers, with whose help he was able to climb the elevation, thus teaching Service.

3. The candidate then was given a bundle of twigs and told to place some on the council fire, where the twigs caught fire and blazed brightly, thus showing Cheerfulness.

Order of the Arrow handclasp

In the first year, 25 members were inducted into the Brotherhood. Many of the members wore a black sash with a white arrow on it. Like the white-on-black insignia worn by the Chief of the Fire and his assistant, the white arrow on the black sash stood out in the light of the council fire. In the original plan there were two degrees; the first was much like a combination of the Ordeal and Brotherhood memberships, and the second an early version of the Vigil Honor.

To perpetuate the Brotherhood, a membership meeting was held on November 23, 1915. George W. Chapman, the first lodge chief of Unami Lodge, served as chairman of the organization committee. This marked the first formal meeting of the Order of the Arrow. Goodman and Edson served as advisers to the committee.

The secret name given the new organization was Wimachtendienk, Wingolauchsik, Witahemui, interpreted from a Lenni Lenape dictionary as the Brotherhood of Cheerful Service. The public name adopted was W.W.W. or the Wimachtendienk (the Brotherhood). Due to another organization using similar letters, the public name was later changed to Wimachtendienk, W.W. before it finally became the Order of the Arrow in 1924.

By 1917, news of the organization spread to other Scout camps and inquiries began. Goodman spoke to many interested Scouts and Scouters, and as a result, lodges were established in New Jersey, Maryland, New York, and Illinois.

From 1915 until 1921 the Order grew slowly. World War I kept Scouts and leaders busy with many other projects. In 1921 steps were taken to establish the Order on a national basis. The early years had produced sufficient experience to form a foundation on sound basic policies.

The first national convention was held on October 7, 1921, in Philadelphia, at which a national lodge was formed, composed of four delegates from each of the local lodges. This group adopted a constitution and a statement of policies. Committees were appointed to develop plans for making the Order effective as a national honor campers' brotherhood.

Following the convention there was a steady growth in lodges and membership. In 1922, after the national lodge meeting at Reading, Pa., the Order of the Arrow became an official program experiment of the Boy Scouts of America.

For several years conventions of the national lodge were held annually. After 1927, they were held at two-year intervals. During the Philadelphia convention of 1929, it was suggested that the Order become an official part of the Boy Scouts of America and a component part of its program. At the session of the national lodge in 1933, held at the Owasippe Camps of the Chicago Council, this proposal was made and ratified by the delegates.

On June 2, 1934, at the National Council Annual Meeting in Buffalo, N.Y., the Order of the Arrow program was approved by the National Council.

While meeting in Seattle, Wash., in May 1948, the Executive Board, upon recommendation of its Committee on Camping, officially integrated the Order of the Arrow into the Scouting movement. The Order's national lodge was dissolved and supervision shifted to the Boy Scouts of America.

The executive committee of the national lodge became the national Committee on Order of the Arrow, a subcommittee of the national Committee on Camping and Engineering, and a staff member was employed as national executive secretary, now the director of the Order of the Arrow. In the 2008 reorganization of the Boy Scouts of America, the national Order of the Arrow committee became a support committee of the national Outdoor Adventures Committee. In 1998, the Order became recognized as Scouting's National Honor Society.

The growth of the Order of the Arrow through the years has never been based on an aggressive promotional plan. It came about because councils believed in the ideals expressed by the Order and voluntarily requested that lodges be formed. The soundness of providing a single workable honor society, rather than many, is evident. More than 2 million Boy Scouts and Scouters have been inducted into the Order during the past 98 years. There are now more than 171,000 active members.

Purpose of the Ordeal

It is the purpose of the Ordeal to have the candidate reflect on his own Scout life and character and come to a deeper understanding of the Scout Oath and the principles of the Order.

Ties of Brotherhood

To become a member of the Order of the Arrow, you had to be selected by vote of the Scouts in your troop or team. Since most of those who selected you for this honor are not members of your lodge, it is easy to see that the membership is controlled by young men in units and not by those who are already members.

Always remember that you were honored by your peers, who elected you to the Order because of your camping ability and Scouting spirit.

They set you apart as one from whom they expect much. They expect you to give leadership in camping and cheerful service.

You must resolve, therefore, not to let them down!

THE ORDEAL

After Order of the Arrow election, a Boy Scout, Varsity Scout, or Scouter is considered a candidate until completion of the Ordeal.

Purpose of the Ordeal. It is the purpose of the Ordeal to have candidates reflect on their own Scout life and character and come to a deeper understanding of the Scout Oath and the principles of the Order. This purpose is realized through a fourfold Ordeal that includes sleeping alone, silence, work, and a limited amount of food.

The candidate spends a night alone as proof of courage and self-reliance. It also gives the individual a chance to think over clearly the events taking place.

The candidate keeps complete silence. This gives him or her the opportunity to pay stricter attention to unspoken thoughts, searching out past deficiencies and resolving on a life of fuller service in the future.

The candidate spends the daylight hours of the Ordeal in meaningful labor. This proves the candidate's willingness to serve others cheerfully.

The candidate also eats sparingly, thus proving the ability to subordinate the appetites of the body to the high purposes of the spirit.

Taken together, the four elements of the Ordeal are a meaningful and inspiring experience for the candidate. They provide a total participation of the mind and spirit. The Ordeal is not soon forgotten by the new member.

Ordeal membership. The steps required to complete the Ordeal membership are defined clearly. Once a person has been elected to the Order of the Arrow by unit members, he or she is formally recognized as a candidate. This is done at a call-out ceremony, usually conducted by the ceremonies team in an outdoor setting. The candidate then takes part in a brief pre-Ordeal ceremony, and then an actual Ordeal (series of tests) to prove sincere dedication to the principles of the Order of the Arrow. Finally, if qualified, the candidate is accepted as a member in a colorful ceremony.

Call-out ceremonies. Many lodges have developed their own call-out ceremonies, which might be done at camp during the evening assembly in the dining hall, or at some other activity and place. Call-out ceremonies also have been developed for camporees and district or council events. The items that must be included in a call-out ceremony are described in the *Guide to Inductions,* which is available for download and printing at *http://www.oa-bsa.org.*

At times the pre-Ordeal and Ordeal ceremonies are held during the evening and night of the day following the call-out. If so, the candidates are instructed in advance by an Ordealmaster. If some time is to elapse before the ceremonies, the following information should be sent by mail to each candidate:

1. Notice that the candidate has been selected by the individual's fellow campers. This should be done regardless of whether the candidate was told at the time of the election.

2. Specific date, place, and time that the candidate should report for the Ordeal.

3. Instructions that the candidate come fully prepared with blankets or sleeping bag and a ground cloth for an overnight campout alone in the open, and a change of clothing suitable for a day's labor.

4. Notice of all costs that the candidate will be expected to pay, including sash, manual, food, etc.

Ordealmaster's job. The Ordealmaster, a young man under the age of 21, is appointed by the lodge chief with the advice of the lodge adviser. He will have charge of the candidates during the pre-Ordeal and Ordeal. He should be a mature member with good judgment and have full authority to make changes in the Ordeal procedure to meet with varying situations, such as severe weather conditions or the candidate's physical condition. A candidate's health should not be endangered by the conditions under which the Ordeal is conducted.

The Ordealmaster must conduct the Ordeal on a high standard with **no hazing.** Extreme care should be taken that each candidate fully understands the symbolism of the pre-Ordeal ceremony and the reason for all Ordeal tests. He makes sure that each candidate knows why he or she spent a night alone, was required to spend a day in silence, and spent the day working.

The entire pre-Ordeal and Ordeal should be conducted in a remote part of camp; if possible, in an area rarely used. No effort should be made to tease or tempt a candidate to break the pledge of silence or to eat more food than officially authorized by the Ordealmaster.

The Scout executive, camp director, and Ordealmaster and assistants have the right to suspend the "no talking" rule should an emergency arise.

Ordeal projects. Meaningful projects should be a concern of the Ordealmaster and his assistants. The candidates should feel that they are making a positive contribution to the camp. Advance planning is a must.

Candidates should be matched with projects they are capable of handling. Be sure that the necessary equipment and supplies are on hand so that no time is lost.

Adult candidates should be given adult-type projects and an adult should be assigned to oversee their Ordeal projects.

Spirit of the Arrow. The *Spirit of the Arrow* pamphlets are a method of preparing Ordeal candidates for membership in the Order of the Arrow.

These pamphlets are a handy aid for Ordeal candidates, enabling them to discover the meaning of their experiences while they are actually taking part in the silent portion of the Ordeal. Lodges using the *Spirit of the Arrow* material report that candidates who use individual booklets do so willingly with fine results.

The *Spirit of the Arrow* pamphlets are a self-training device that helps the candidate understand the deepest and most inspirational meanings of the Ordeal. The pamphlets are given to the candidates at specified times during and after the Ordeal. The pamphlets are a resource in the *Guide to Inductions,* available for download and printing at *http://www.oa-bsa.org.*

The Ordeal and the induction. Just as the induction is at the heart of the Order, the Ordeal is at the heart of the induction. You first experienced the Order in the Ordeal. You lived our principles and traditions. At the same time, existing members recharged themselves. Now, your study and application of the Ordeal's lessons guide you. Thus, the Ordeal was not only your conduit into the Order, it will remain a channel for your Order of the Arrow experiences.

Begin now by recalling your own Ordeal. Then read this section to compare your experience with that of thousands of Arrowmen before you. Finally, decide how to use your new understanding.

Evening of the pre-Ordeal. After check-in and probably a long wait, you were taken to a strange clearing in the woods. At the center of a circle was an unlit fire. Light came from 15 blazes forming the circle and representing the Scout Oath and Law.

Four figures in ceremonial attire stood around the fire lay. Kichkinet, in the East, is your guide in the ceremonies. He symbolizes leadership. Nutiket, in the South, is the guard of the circle. He upholds the tradition of cheerfulness. Meteu, in the West, is the medicine man and represents brotherhood. He reminds us to love one another. Allowat Sakima, in the North, is the mighty chief, and exemplifies service.

Each one spoke to you. Nutiket told of the scant food test. He flexed a bow as a token of liveliness and flexibility under stress, the principle of Cheerfulness. He then gave the bow to Allowat Sakima. Meteu pledged you to silence and displayed a bowstring as a token of the ties of Brotherhood. He also passed the token to Allowat Sakima.

Allowat Sakima spoke of the day of work and strung the bow uniting Brotherhood and Cheerfulness. He was wearing a quiver of arrows representing the burden of service he carries as chief. He drew one arrow from the quiver as a token that your election separated you from your fellow Scouts for something higher. He asked you to test the bow to show your willingness to try your dedication to Scout ideals. Lastly, Kichkinet shot the arrow upward, symbolizing the pathway you follow if your dedication is unwavering. He told of your need to spend the night alone. Saying, "Let us try to find the Arrow!" he led you away from the circle.

Your guide set you out alone for the night. In the future you will separate yourself. As a leader, you will occasionally make unpopular decisions. You may need to "leave the crowd and its opinions." This will be hard and unpleasant, and others may treat you roughly. Again, you can show the courage that you demonstrated on your night alone. You can rescue yourself from complete isolation with the self-reliance you used when your guide set you apart.

Day of the Ordeal. You pledged yourself to silence for the Ordeal. Did you notice how the silence bound you to the other candidates and made you more aware of their needs? The Ordeal illustrates the value of getting away from the noisy confusion of life. Time in thoughtful silence helps you with difficult decisions. When you have an important choice, stop and listen. We all make mistakes. But most errors occur when we rush off without hearing our inner voice.

Your day of work showed your willingness to serve, even when service involves hardship and toil, or seems dumb and boring. In the Ordeal you had help and cooperation from others, but in Scouting and daily life, you will often serve without them. Prepare to give more difficult service, like befriending a Scout others are teasing.

The scant food test illustrates self-denial. You will abandon personal comfort and momentary desires to achieve goals. On your quest do not merely help others, but do so willingly and cheerfully. When uncomfortable or frustrated, when giving up a personal desire, this test challenges again.

Just as you did all four tests—isolation, silence, arduous labor, and scant food—together during the Ordeal, you will find them useful together in daily life. Consider silence and isolation. You need time alone every day. Some Arrowmen use a few minutes to review their Good Turns and misdeeds each day, guided by their sense of right and wrong. Then they set goals and make plans. Thinking alone without the noisy intrusions of the outside world joins the tests of silence and isolation. You should maintain a regular habit of taking stock of yourself alone with your God.

Evening of the Ordeal. As on the previous evening, you were taken to a special place. This time, however, you placed a hand on the shoulder of the Scout in front of you. This was a token of your intention to continue in service to your troop or team. Then you were bound by a rope representing brotherhood. Finally, you advanced toward the fire of cheerfulness. With these three acts you prepared symbolically to receive the Obligation of the Order.

After you took upon yourself your solemn Obligation, Meteu gave you the legend of how the Order was founded. He spoke of the peaceful Lenni Lenape (the Delaware Indians), their chief, Chingachgook, and the chief's son, Uncas. When war threatened, Chingachgook sought volunteers to alert other villages, but few saw danger. Most were apathetic, only wanting to enjoy their life at home. However, Uncas had a higher vision of life. He cheerfully offered his help despite the negative attitudes around him. He cared enough for others that he was willing to face hardship and life-threatening danger, alone if necessary.

Uncas, Chingachgook, and others with like motives gave self-sacrificing service, and the fierce marauders were compelled to retire to their own country. When peace returned, to maintain and spread the shared vision of cheerful service, Chingachgook bound Uncas and those who joined him together as brothers. The Lenni Lenape named this brotherhood Wimachtendienk, Wingolauchsik, Witahemui. Today, you carry on its traditions in the Order of the Arrow.

Allowat Sakima then described the Arrow as being "straight, its point keen. Aimed high, its course is undeviating, its direction onward and upward." He whispered a single word in your ear, our Admonition, which is the key to the Order. He also gave you the Order of the Arrow handclasp with his left hand, as in the Scout handclasp, intertwining the third and fourth fingers. The two interlocked fingers represent the bonds of Brotherhood. Finally, you received your Ordeal sash.

Ordeal sash

Keeping the legend of the Order alive. Do you hope to serve your community? Can you make a contribution such as that made by Uncas and Chingachgook? "Neighboring tribes and distant enemies" may not seem to threaten your "peaceful way of life." Yet the challenges are there for farsighted leaders to find and attack. Will you play the role of Chingachgook who first saw the problem and sounded the alarm? Or of Uncas who cheerfully offered his services when others would not? Or will you hide in the nameless crowd?

Dedicated people continue to make admirable contributions to humanity through lifetimes of cheerful, self-sacrificing service. Mohandas Gandhi led the nonviolent movement for freedom of the Indian subcontinent. Albert Schweitzer gave medical service in Africa. Dietrich Bonhoffer preached and acted against Hitler within Nazi Germany. Martin Luther King Jr. led the American civil rights movement. Each led a life worthy of your study. Each was controversial in his day. Each, in his own way, espoused the principles of the Order and lived the tests of the Ordeal. Who of your heroes could you add to this group? For each of the prominent people who can be named as having led a worthy life of service to others, tens of thousands, indeed millions, of others have likewise made a difference. You can be one of these. How will future generations judge your contribution?

Mystery and the Ordeal. As a member of the Order, you have undergone tests and ceremonies that challenged you and helped you to think about your life. The mystery in which we cloak these steps is part of the induction. Candidates receive less benefit if they know about the induction in advance. Most candidates feel anxiety about the unknown as they approach the Ordeal. Knowledge lowers expectancy, dulls the edge of experience. In other words, you hurt candidates when you tell them about the Ordeal. They are better off knowing nothing until they receive the challenges from the age-old figures in the pre-Ordeal ceremony.

Be vague when answering questions from Scouts and Scouters about the Ordeal. Do not even confirm or deny what they think they know. Smiling pleasantly (as you remember the great time you had!) and changing the subject is best. Leaving a sense of mystery adds to the Order of the Arrow for everyone. You have earned the right to learn about the Order, including the Ordeal; those who have not been elected have not. Exposing our special ceremonial details is unfair to everyone.

Stretching the truth or just plain lying about the Order or the Ordeal is not Scoutlike. If you cause a candidate to worry about something that is not part of the Ordeal, you have distracted the individual from the purpose. And that hurts everyone!

On the other hand, the Order of the Arrow recognizes the right of interested adults to learn about our purpose and methods. Youths should feel free to discuss their experiences with their parents.

Attending the Ordeal as a member. Every Ordeal requires detailed planning, extensive training, and careful preparation. Presenting a good one is difficult and complex. It must go so smoothly that the candidates are not aware of the complex administrative details.

Personifying the role of Allowat Sakima, Meteu, Nutiket, or Kichkinet is a rewarding job. But it requires commitment. Memorization is easy only if you begin months ahead. Team members study the meanings of the lines, practice delivery and movements, and become emotionally involved in conveying the message to the candidates.

Serving as an Elangomat, "friend" in the language of the Lenni Lenape, is also rewarding and challenging. As an Elangomat, you go through the tests of the Ordeal along with the candidates. Your example is a better teacher of Brotherhood, Cheerfulness, and Service than any spoken words. By learning more about the Order and yourself, you also rededicate yourself to the Order. Dedication to the ideals of the Order is the hallmark of a good Elangomat.

Each Elangomat generally leads a patrol-size group of candidates, often called a "clan." When the lodge uses them, each clan is independent from the others. Since an Elangomat shares the test of silence and cannot easily ask questions, the lodge trains him in advance. During the Ordeal, the lodge provides him with close support to meet any needs.

A successful Ordeal also has many behind-the-scenes contributors. Brothers cook food, prepare sashes and supplies, complete records, issue membership cards, build and extinguish fires, and so on. Many helpful members make a complete Ordeal.

Every member must be an Elangomat at times. We have grown in understanding since our Ordeals. We recognize the significance of the tests more than at first. Thus, when near candidates, we share the tests wholeheartedly. A spirit of seriousness and commitment, seen by the candidates in each member, shows them that the tests are not a joke or harassment but an important pointer to a valuable way of life.

Compliance with the Ordeal. From the time of election through the pre-Ordeal and Ordeal, including the Ordeal ceremony, all candidates should be able to qualify for all the tests of the Ordeal. Rarely is there a violation of the spirit of the Ordeal so flagrant as to make a candidate unworthy. When this happens the candidate usually withdraws without being asked, because he or she realizes personal shortcomings.

The Ordealmaster should report all violations to a lodge adviser or camp director, who may wish to discuss the matter privately with the candidate involved. It must be remembered that the lodge members cannot vote to accept or reject candidates properly elected by their fellow campers.

Why ceremonies? The ceremonies of the Order of the Arrow were developed to help members learn and be inspired to fulfill the Order's high purpose. They are not meant to imitate the induction procedures of adult fraternal groups. The following policy on safeguarding all ceremonial concepts and materials should be exercised.

Youth and adult candidates for membership into the Order of the Arrow are introduced to the Order's concepts of servant leadership through a safeguarded ceremonial induction. Nonmembers should not attend the ceremonies.

Although the content of the ceremonies is private, the ceremonies were designed to avoid offending any religious belief and have received the approval of religious leaders. The ceremonies are consistent with Scouting traditions and the spirit of the Scout Oath and Law.

The Order of the Arrow recognizes and respects the right of any parent, Scout leader, or religious leader to be interested in the content of the ceremony. The lodge adviser, or his designee, may discuss the content of the ceremony and any other issues brought to his attention by one of these interested and responsible adults, with the understanding that the adult will maintain the confidentiality of the ceremony.

If after discussing the ceremony with the lodge adviser, the parent, Scout leader, or religious leader continues to have questions about the content of the ceremony, that person will be permitted to read the ceremony text. Following this, parents will be in a position to decide whether to allow their son to participate in the ceremony. Candidates may not become members of the Order of the Arrow without completing the pre-Ordeal and Ordeal ceremonies.

YOU AND YOUR UNIT

Your unit. An Arrowman's primary responsibility is to the troop or team. It was your fellow Scouts who elected you to membership in the Order and it is to them that you should devote most of your service.

Your fellow Scouts elected you to membership because of your Scout spirit, service to Scouting, and camping ability. They set you apart as one from whom they expect a great deal. Your experience with the Ordeal should enable you now to give the leadership they want and expect from you. For this reason, your first duty as an Arrowman is to continue to expand your service to your unit. The success of the Order in your unit depends mainly on what you do individually. Your example of cheerful service in camp and at unit meetings is the spark that brings the spirit alive!

Dr. E. Urner Goodman, founder of the Order, once said: "Let it be remembered that the Order of the Arrow was created to help the unit—to help it present its membership a better idea of the inner qualities of the good Scout camper.

"Qualities of character, like cheerfulness and service, are hard for a boy or a man to understand in the abstract. They come easier when seen in human life.

"The Order was started to help glorify these qualities of the good Scout camper in the unit, so that they might be appreciated there, not only during the brief term in summer camp but all of the days and the weeks of the year.

"Let us realize the significance of the Order in the unit—for the unit is our best hope in Scouting . . ."

What are your responsibilities to your unit? Are you the Order of the Arrow troop or team representative? You should make sure that your unit maintains an active camping program and that as many members of the unit as possible are involved. Be sure your lodge or chapter camp promotion team visits your unit at least once a year and that you have an annual Order of the Arrow election for membership. Your unit should help the lodge give service to as many community service projects as possible. It is also important that you keep your unit members informed on current happenings of the lodge and local council.

You were a leader in your troop or team before the Scouts elected you to the Order. Your membership does not change your position in your unit, but the Order does affect your relationship to it. As an Arrowman, you have new responsibilities to your troop or team and a different point of view.

Setting the example. Example setting is central to the methods of the Order. The members of your unit elected you because they look up to you. Your job is to live up to their high expectations—to serve them by being the best example of the Scout Oath and Law in action that you possibly can. As a member of

Scouting's National Honor Society, each Arrowman should set the example by properly wearing the Scout uniform at all Scouting functions.

The Scout Oath and Law are the center of Scouting. But they are mere words for new Scouts until they see these ideals in the actions of unit leaders. This means YOU! How much will "trustworthy" mean if they see you cheat to give your patrol more points? How much will "helpful" mean if you don't work with them on advancement? Or "cheerful" if you get angry when the weather turns bad on a campout or you get stuck with an extra turn of cleaning the dishes?

None of us is perfect. The Order helps us to remind each other that younger Scouts imitate us. We each strive to listen to our personal sense of right and wrong so that others will see a good Scout in action. By electing you to the Order, they entrusted you with this important task. *Don't let them down.*

Leadership in your unit. As your interest in the welfare of your unit and in its members grows, you will take on more difficult leadership roles. You may move up to higher positions in the unit or accept increasingly harder jobs. You may become the Order of the Arrow troop or team representative for your unit. As an Arrowman, do not just take on more, but look for unwanted, yet necessary, tasks. Seek ways to offer friendship and brotherhood as you lead. Maintain a cheerful outlook no matter how difficult the situation.

You need special skills as you endeavor to lead your troop or team in an ethical manner. Giving friendship, running meetings fairly, helping a friend solve problems, sharing skills with others, and building a camping unit, all help you as you lead and as you complete your personal quest.

OA troop/team representative. A youth Arrowman may wish to assume a visible role in maintaining an effective relationship between his unit and the lodge or chapter by serving as an OA troop or team representative. The OA troop or team representative serves as a formal communication and programmatic link to both Arrowmen and nonmembers in the unit, making sure they are aware of chapter and lodge news and activities. He also teaches Scout skills, promotes Scout camping and spirit, sets the example, and encourages Arrowmen in the unit to be active in the lodge and seal their membership in the Order by becoming Brotherhood members. The OA representative is an optional youth leadership position *in the unit* that is appointed by the senior patrol leader or team captain with the approval of the Scoutmaster or Coach. A more detailed job description, duties, and qualifications of the OA troop/team representative may be found on the Order of the Arrow's official website.

Like other youth leadership positions in the unit, the OA troop/team representative is eligible to wear the respective badge of office. The OA troop/team representative is an official youth leadership position of the Boy Scouts of America that can be used for rank advancement.

Giving friendship. All you will do as an Arrowman starts with giving friendship. In turn, your friendship arises from your basic values. Your religious beliefs and moral convictions influence all you think and say and do. Thus, your friendship should be morally sound, predictably strong, and respectful of others. All this makes your gift of friendship invaluable. It will often return to you greatly increased, but don't limit or stunt friendship by giving it only in expectation of return.

Be so constant in your friendship that others can predict your actions in any given situation. When you smile every day at your teachers, they can expect a cheerful outlook during final exams. When you make a new Scout comfortable at his first troop meetings, he can expect to feel at home on his first campout. When you react calmly to small problems, your friends ask you for help in an emergency.

Respect the rights and beliefs of others. Treasure the differences. Learn to enjoy the company of those who are unlike you. Try to generate light rather than heat when discussing politics, religion, or other value-laden subjects. If a friend's behavior bothers you, tell him or her, but never question the sincerity of your friend's motives.

Do not go along when others suggest anything that you consider wrong. Attempt, if you wish, to persuade them that their actions will be wrong. But if necessary, distance yourself from them until another day.

As you practice giving friendship, you master the mechanics that are part of it. Many of them are points of the Scout Law. Smile whenever you can. Learn the names of those you meet and use their names often when talking with them. (Remembering names is work, but it shows your sincerity.) Actively listen to others and encourage them to talk about themselves and their interests. Do not turn private conversations into gossip. Take your burden and then some when there is work to be done. Promptly thank others for any kindness. Encourage bystanders to participate. Each of these are valuable habits of giving friendship, and each of the following sections has more.

Cultivate the habits of giving friendship. Right now can you pick your strongest habit of friendship? What is your weakest habit of friendship?

At the end of each day, review these two habits. Recall the events of the day and ask yourself: When was I especially good at each habit? When was I especially bad? What was different about me that made me act properly one time and poorly the other? How will I try to do better tomorrow? When you have improved both habits, choose two more and improve them the same way.

Through conscious daily effort you can make a good habit part of yourself or break a bad habit. As long as your friendship rises from deeply held convictions, it shows.

Hints on helping a friend in need. Knowing that you are a decent, trustworthy person, someone may turn to you for help when troubled or when he or she has a problem. Be open to help. Give your friend a chance to speak with you alone. Respect your friend's right to privacy.

Be careful not to seem critical; be a friend, not a judge. Picture yourself in your friend's situation and try to understand how he or she feels.

If your friend has done something wrong, don't moralize. Once your friend realizes his or her mistake, he or she needs to figure out how to set it right. Don't kick your friend while he or she is down; help your friend up.

Whether a person has a problem to solve or just needs to talk, a friend can help most by just listening. Let your friend do most of the talking. Encourage your friend to explain himself or herself fully. Explaining a problem often solves it.

Avoid giving advice. People who have problems must arrive at their own decision, one that is right for them. You may make suggestions to help your friend start thinking clearly and creatively. Encourage your friend to think of many possible solutions, even wild ones. But don't push or pretend you have the answers. Your friend will probably resist advice, even if correct. Your friend will have more self-confidence with the decision made if he or she reaches it himself or herself after considering many alternatives.

Be a mirror, not a judge or a know-it-all.

Suppose a friend *tells* you that he or she is involved in something that is not Scout-like. Because you do not discuss private conversations with non-participants, you are on the spot. First, make sure the facts are clear to both you and your friend. Second, encourage your friend to take corrective action. Finally, if others are endangered and your friend does not take corrective action, you must take common-sense action. Go to a parent, Scout leader, religious leader, or another adult you trust for more help.

Every time you discuss a problem with a friend think about it afterward. How did you give solid, supportive friendship? What habits of friendship did you use? What pitfalls mentioned above did you fall into? What alternative solutions did you help your friend explore? What, if any, commitments did you make?

Hints on how to teach a skill to a Scout. Before you attempt to teach a skill to someone else, test yourself. Your mental or written answers will help you teach more successfully. How does the Scout literature describe the skill? What are the safety practices? What are three ways the Scout can apply the skill? Did you follow safety practices? Do you need practice before teaching?

First: Get the Scout to understand how much he does and doesn't know. Stir his curiosity while you discover his skill level. Ask him if he can do the skill, and if he says yes, give him a chance to show you. Adjust your plan to his skill level.

Second: Show him how to do it. Don't just talk. Show him how, slowly. Have him watch from a different angle as you show him again. Point out safety rules as you go.

Third: Let him do it. Help only as needed. But watch carefully.

Fourth: Let him test himself—have him do it without help. Make it a game!

Finally: When you are all done, evaluate your own performance. What evidence is there that you both had a good time? What part of the skill do you need to polish up on? What did you do that most maintained his attention? What goofs do you want to avoid next time? What could he do when you started? When you finished?

Ask your troop or team leaders for as many instructor assignments as possible; one for every meeting is not too many. Occasionally, ask someone you consider a good instructor to observe from a distance and evaluate your efforts. As you gain confidence ask the Scout for his evaluation of your teaching. The more you think about and work at teaching, the better an instructor you will become.

Unit camping traditions. Developing and maintaining camping traditions is one of the purposes of the Order. Every good Scout troop or team has special camping traditions of its own. Traditions help bind the unit together from year to year. They add quality and sparkle to the troop program. Scouts like them, and anticipate having the same fun they had last time.

Here are examples of traditions from across the nation. Each is a source of deep pride for those units that follow it. You may find some a bit unusual, but use them to stimulate your imagination.

- Go camping every month.

- Attend summer camp each year.

- Go on a survival camping trip every August.

- Never camp twice in the same place within a year.

- Have a long weekend backpacking trip twice a year.

- Always cook by patrol, even at resident camp.

- Never call off a camping trip because of bad weather, except hurricane, tornado, or blizzard.

- Have a special 50-miler each year for those Scouts meeting requirements in attendance or advancement set by the troop.

- Once each year each patrol has its own campout.

- Do a service project for a local hiking trail as part of a camping trip each year.

- Always cook breakfast and supper from scratch.

- Hike every marked trail at resident camp each summer.

- Give each patrol a distinct campsite, slightly apart from the others.

- Always hike into the campsite.

- Work on advancement on every campout, even camporees.

- Hold a snow camping trip each year.

- Always camp in ponchos, never in tents.

- Take a hike on every campout.

- Have patrol competition on each campout.

- Watch sunrise or sunset from a special spot.

- Visit the national Scout jamboree as a troop.

YOU AND YOUR LODGE

Your lodge. Members of the Order of the Arrow are organized into groups called "lodges." Each lodge has its own name and distinctive emblem, called a totem.

The Order became an official part of Scouting in 1948. The Boy Scouts of America charters only one lodge per council. The council must recharter its lodge annually.

The council administers the Order of the Arrow as part of its camping program. The Scout executive is the Supreme Chief of the Fire, the final authority within the council for the Order of the Arrow. Annually, the Scout executive appoints the adult leader of the lodge, the lodge adviser, who serves as Deputy Supreme Chief of the Fire. The lodge adviser acts on behalf of the Scout executive in guiding the day-to-day affairs of the lodge. Other advisers are appointed to assist the lodge adviser in carrying out responsibilities. Optionally, an associate lodge adviser may be appointed to assist the lodge adviser. Because of the burden of responsibilities, the Scout executive may delegate duties with the lodge to another professional staff member as lodge staff adviser.

The Order of the Arrow is a program designed for youth. All lodge and chapter officers and committee chairmen *must* be under the age of 21 during their entire term of office. Adults serve in advisory capacities only. The officers plan and conduct all meetings and events, as well as develop and fund an annual operating budget.

The Scout executive may choose to divide the lodge into chapters. In such cases, often there is one chapter for each district. Each chapter has its own officers and advisers. Like the lodge, all chapter officers and committee chairmen must be younger than 21 during their entire term of office. In this case, the Scout executive annually appoints a chapter adviser and chapter staff adviser (who normally is a district executive).

Each lodge (and chapter) is run by the youth members, under 21 years of age. Only those younger than 21 may hold office or vote on any action. Elected lodge officers include the chief, one or more vice chiefs, a secretary, and a treasurer. The lodge chief appoints a chairman for each lodge committee—both permanent operating committees and temporary committees created from time to time. Chapters have a similar structure. Adults serve as advisers to each youth position as described under "The Scouter's Role," found later in this chapter.

Your lodge has annual dues that pay for mailing newsletters, annual registration of the lodge, and other necessary lodge expenses. Your first year's dues were probably included in your Ordeal fee. The lodge newsletter will remind you each year of your annual dues and may allow you to pay by mail. You may also be able to pay at lodge activities or at your council service center.

Your lodge has formal, written rules that give the details of its structure. They usually specify offices, operating committees, lodge dues, and makeup of the executive committee. Following the rules, the lodge executive committee plans and carries out the lodge program. The entire lodge may vote on major decisions.

You may expect to receive several issues of your lodge newsletter a year. Rather than mailing at regular intervals, lodges tend to send out newsletters before activities. However, if you haven't received anything in four months, you may not be on the mailing list. Check with any chapter or lodge officer or the council service center. Because meetings of the entire lodge membership are infrequent, lodge records are much more difficult to maintain properly than troop or team records. Your council or lodge may also have an Internet website with news, information, and announcements about upcoming activities.

Lodge (or chapter) events each year include one or more Ordeals, some weekends of service, fun, and fellowship, and perhaps an annual banquet. Most weekends include an opportunity for you to complete Brotherhood membership. Ask your Order of the Arrow troop or team representative about these events and opportunities. Get together with other Arrowmen in your unit and nearby units to arrange transportation.

Lodge and chapter responsibilities. The division of labor between a lodge and its chapters varies widely. Here is a typical split to suggest how and where you might participate.

What lodges typically do:

- Make long-range plans, including budgets.
- Make operating policy decisions.
- Keep membership and financial records.
- Collect dues; order and sell supplies.
- Develop camping promotions and unit elections materials.
- Lead participation in sectional and national events.
- Publish a lodge newsletter.
- Make Vigil Honor and Founder's Award nominations and handle other awards.
- Provide leadership training.
- Plan, run, and evaluate lodge activities.
- Provide liaison to the local council.

What chapters typically do:

- Supervise Order of the Arrow elections in the geographical area.
- Hold several meetings each year.
- Act as a rallying point for members going to lodge activities.
- Support a specialized part of the lodge program (such as a ceremonial or dance team).
- Have specific jobs at lodge activities, such as cooking and cleanup, etc.
- Write for the lodge newsletter or its own newsletter.

A good chapter does one or two of these each year:

- Conduct a service project.
- Provide support at a camporee or Scout show.
- Perform American Indian dances and conduct ceremonies for Cub Scout packs.
- Have a call-out ceremony.

In some large lodges, chapters are like "minilodges" and may do the following:

- Hold one or more Ordeals a year.
- Hold one or more Brotherhood ceremonies a year.

Service in the lodge. You are invited and encouraged to participate in lodge meetings and projects. The lodge has opportunities for additional service in many areas, some of which are listed here:

- Camping promotion visits to troops and teams
- Publishing a "Where to Go Camping" booklet or Internet website
- Weekend camp improvement projects
- Sponsorship of youth leader training programs
- Conducting Order of the Arrow elections in units
- Conducting campfires and call-out ceremonies

Your participation in lodge activities will help you become acquainted with a project or committee in which you can serve actively.

Committees. The lodge executive committee is the steering committee of the Order of the Arrow program within the local council. To get the work done, the lodge is organized into committees. Suggested committees include: service, finance, unit elections, ceremonial, membership, and camping promotion. Lodge activity depends on the enthusiastic service of its members. Therefore, the lodge should seek to make committee work interesting and see to it that members are invited to serve on committees that interest them and that committee meetings are held at convenient times and places.

The methods of the Order. Since the earliest days of the Order, its officers and committees have made decisions based on sound methods of operation. You have read many of these earlier, but they are all here for your review. How have these methods affected your experience with the Order? How can you use them if you become more active in the Order?

- **Importance of the individual.** The Ordeal accomplishes its purpose through the individual actions of each Arrowman. Each Brother's spiritual and moral values, especially as stated in the Scout Oath and Law, are at the heart of the experience in the Order.

- **Importance of camping.** The outdoor program of Scouting produces self-reliant citizens. Arrowmen work toward more Scouts camping and having a better experience.

- **Setting the example.** Qualities of character, like brotherhood, cheerfulness, and service, are hard to understand in the abstract. They come easier when seen in human life. Each Arrowman's example is the main service of the Order to Scouting.

- **Induction sequence.** Introduction to the principles of the Order occurs in an orderly manner over several months. Each Arrowman grows through a similar pattern of ceremonies, service, and reflection.

- **Role of ceremony.** Ceremonies present the principles of the Order in an exciting and impressive atmosphere. They enable the members to be more effective in setting the example.

- **Role of mystery.** Arrowmen maintain an air of mystery about the Order and its ceremonies because of the attractive role mystery plays. To maintain mystery, the Order restricts the pre-Ordeal and Ordeal ceremonies to candidates and members. Other ceremonies of the Order are conducted the same way. However, concerned adults may easily learn about the Order through the lodge adviser.

- **Democratic selection of members.** Full membership in the Order is an honor granted to a Scout by those who know him the best, the Scouts of his troop. All Scouts in the troop may vote in this election.

- **Forward looking.** Membership in the Order is not given for past accomplishments. Scouting expects each Arrowman to continue growth and service.

- **Equality of membership.** Lodge membership entitles an Arrowman to all its rights and privileges.

- **Operation of program by youth.** Members under 21 plan and operate the program of the lodge. Members 21 and older may not vote. The Scout executive appoints adults as advisers and as supreme chief of the fire has ultimate authority.

- **Democratic internal operation.** Lodge rules, adopted by the lodge youth membership, govern its affairs. Following these rules, officers are elected by vote of these members.

- **Part of the Boy Scouts of America.** The Order of the Arrow has no existence apart from Scouting. It is a device used in Scouting's camping program. The lodge is part of the local council and under the administrative authority of the Scout executive. Registered membership in the Boy Scouts of America is a requirement for membership in the Order.

Lodge membership. Members of the Order of the Arrow may be official dues-paying (and in the case of youth, voting) members of only one lodge, that being the lodge chartered to the council where they reside and have their principal Scouting registration. Members may only wear the lodge pocket flap of the lodge where their dues are paid.

It is acceptable for an Arrowman to maintain contact with a lodge where he or she was formerly a member, and he or she is welcome to pay a fee to receive communication from his or her former lodge if that lodge so permits. However, this former member of the lodge cannot vote and should not attempt to influence lodge policy inasmuch as he or she is a guest or visitor, not an official dues-paying member of the lodge. This person cannot hold any office or position or wear the lodge pocket flap.

Arrowmen with extended residence away from their normal home, such as students living away from home at school or members of the military, may maintain their Order of the Arrow membership in either place, but not both. An Arrowman who desires to join the lodge away from home must also register in the BSA local council for that location. The Order is an integral part of Scouting, and we all owe primary responsibility to Scouting wherever we are members of the Order.

YOU AND YOUR LOCAL COUNCIL

Your local council. Your lodge serves as an important part of your local council operation. It aids the council not only with the camping program, but provides meaningful service to the council when needed.

The lodge works with the council camping committee in coordinating its yearly projects and activities. It is recommended that one of the lodge officers sit on the council camping committee to keep open the lines of communication. The lodge adviser should serve as a member of the camping committee to coordinate the annual programs of the lodge with the objectives of the committee.

Camping promotion. As Scouting's National Honor Society, one of the lodge's basic objectives is to promote the camping program of the local council. This should include troop and team visitation by members of the lodge or chapter camping promotion committee. Each Arrowman should become the camping promoter in his or her own unit.

Camping provided the environment for you to learn to work as a member of a group, to discover new places and friends, and to grow by becoming aware of your abilities. Because you learned these lessons, your unit elected you to the Order. In your Ordeal, camping again provided the time and place for growth.

Your task now is to enhance the camping program of your troop or team so that other Scouts learn, discover, and grow as you did. This may seem difficult, since the goal is vague and the effect of your efforts hard to observe. But, here are some effective ways to improve camping that can make a real difference.

- Encourage camping. As a member of the Order of the Arrow, you are a respected member of your unit. Other Scouts look up to you. Thus you can enhance camping by simply supporting patrol and unit campouts enthusiastically. Your enthusiasm for camping—especially when things aren't going right—can make a tremendous difference in how others feel about it.

- Improve your camping skills. Can you identify most of the trees you see while camping? Can you start a fire with flint and steel? Do you always wash your dishes properly? Do you use topographic maps often enough to use them well? You can learn a lot from the *Boy Scout Handbook* and the *Fieldbook*. To become good at a skill, you may need to do some library research or to find someone (perhaps another Arrowman) who can give you some pointers. This is part of the fun. But above all, practice! You can't be an expert at everything. But you can find one or two skills that aren't well-known in your unit and learn all you can about them. Once you know them, use these skills often and enthusiastically.

- Help new Scouts with camping skills and jobs. Camping isn't fun if you don't know how. Show a new Scout how to enjoy his first campout—how to make a comfortable bed on the ground, cook a hearty meal, start a fire, and track a bird or animal. You will find that teaching helps sharpen your own camping skills.

  There are always tasks that no one enjoys: hauling water, washing dishes, latrine duty. If you are in charge, make sure these tasks are fairly divided. Don't ask a Scout to do more than he is physically able.

  Five gallons of water (about 40 pounds) is a lot to carry for a Scout who weighs little more. If a task must be done in a certain way, make sure the Scout knows it. Finally, as an Arrowman, you should enthusiastically help new Scouts with these tasks.

- Encourage variety in camping. Look for new places to camp, and suggest a variety of campout themes and activities. Talk to Arrowmen in other units and read BSA and other camping literature for ideas. If your parents belong to an auto club, ask them to get you the club's camping guide for the area. Encourage your troop or team to try new, exciting, and different types of camping experiences by making detailed suggestions.

- Promote good camping traditions. Does your unit have any camping traditions? Things that make your troop or team special? Don't let them be forgotten over the years. Think about the best times you've had while camping with your unit. Make sure the new Scouts have similar experiences. When your troop or team does something that makes everyone feel proud, suggest creating a new tradition around it.

  On the other hand, do your best to discourage undesirable traditions. Initiations, teasing, or harassment of new Scouts have no place in a Scout camp. Even the traditional campfire ghost story can make sleeping away from the comforts of home a scary proposition. Small incidents that make Scouts unhappy can sour them on camping and undo all your positive efforts.

- Promote camping personally. Notice which members of the unit go camping and which do not. Without getting pushy, talk to a Scout who isn't camping and try to find out why he chooses not to. Perhaps he has a problem to resolve (like the ghost story mentioned above). Showing concern often is enough to make a difference.

- Go camping. Don't just talk about it. Go!

Summer camp promotion. To be successful in sales, you must believe in your product. You can't sell summer camp unless you believe in camp yourself. Spend some silent time alone thinking about what you like about camp and the great times you have had.

- Put up an attractive camping poster in your troop or team meeting room. You might want to feature pictures of your unit at summer camp. Such a poster is a weekly visual reminder of the fun you had at summer camp. When a Scout commits to going, have him sign up. Make sure that your name is at the head of the list. The earlier you start, the better. The first troop or team meeting in September is not too early if a Scout works to pay his own way.

Annually, the Order of the Arrow provides a free Camp Promotion Kit to every troop and team in the country. For more information about the kit, contact your local council service center or the Order of the Arrow at the national office.

- Ask each member if he is going to camp. Some wouldn't miss it for anything; they're already sold. Recognize their commitment and show them sincere appreciation. Then call on them to encourage others. Some will never go; you're seeking those Scouts who aren't sure. List these Scouts as you find them. When you have several you are ready to achieve success.

- Talk to each Scout privately. Find out what his interests are. Discover why he is hesitant about going. Are his friends going? Will there be others his age going? Is there something he has heard about camp that worries him?

Remember that a Scout goes to camp for a good time. Stories of your good times are the best evidence of fun at camp. Don't try to sell him the whole camp. Find out what he likes, and sell him those parts of camp that appeal to him. When he believes he will have fun, he'll decide to go. Even if he doesn't go, if you do it right, you will have given friendship. And that's worthwhile.

OA Mentoring Program. Arrowmen have a special opportunity to assist the camping and advancement programs of Scout units needing help. The Order of the Arrow Mentoring Program was established in 2000 as a joint effort with the BSA Multicultural Markets Team. Arrowmen are encouraged to serve as positive change agents and role models for Scouts and leaders in urban and rural units.

To become an OA mentor, Arrowmen must develop an action plan that is approved by the lodge leadership, the district commissioner and the selected urban/rural unit leadership. Three to five mentors (adult/youth combination) should be assigned to the selected unit for at least a three-month period. At the end of the mentoring period, the unit should be left with confirmed commissioner service and be charged with assisting another unit in need.

Scout campfires. The campfire has been a focal point in Scouting since the days when Robert Baden-Powell invented Scout camping on Brownsea Island. Whether at the patrol campsite or in the dim evening shadows of the Ordeal, the spirit of Scouting is born in the fire and carried on its smoke. Songs, skits, stories, and silly yells tie each Scout to the tradition of cheerfulness. The fire itself directs the pageantry and symbolizes the day's activities, beginning with its lively crackling start, through a period of bright light and merriment, yielding slowly to a glow of embers.

A successful campfire requires planning and organization. A few key activities provide the framework for a memorable evening. Just as no two fires are built of identical wood, no two scripts should be the same. However, they have similar parts whether the group is large or small, old friends or new. After the opening is a lively period of fun and Scout songs as we use our own energy to excite the flames. As the fire burns low we enjoy a slower time of soft-spoken stories, songs, dreams, and memories as we relax in the satisfaction of a completed day.

The closing of the campfire instills the flame of Scouting in each Scout and ends the day with a moment of inspiration and reverence.

The *Boy Scout Handbook* and the *Fieldbook* both discuss fire building and fire safety. The log-cabin or council fire lay is the best for campfires. You can change the fire size to match the group size. The base of the fire is three or four layers of split, well-dried wood. (Mix quick- and slow-burning woods if the program will be lengthy and the woods are available.) A tepee fire is often built on top of the well-packed lower layers. The quick-starting tepee fire establishes an initial mood of cheerfulness, and its coals catch the lower layers.

The campfire is a symbolic meeting place and a source of light. The audience can see the action any place around a small fire. Thus, it is better than a raging inferno. For a campfire for a large group, use two fires with a distance of about 15 feet between them. If you raise the fires on two fireproof platforms, you provide even better lighting.

Some folks think that a proper campfire requires the smell of kerosene. However, for the sake of safety, limit artificial materials in the fire to wax or paper. Dramatic fire lightings are fun, but make sure they are safe and will work. Always have an alternate plan. Have the fire going well as the first Scouts enter the campfire circle. You then can have your opening ceremony well lit and focus on the message of the ceremony rather than the mechanics of getting the fire to go.

The *Troop Program Resources* has hints on ceremonies and Scoutmaster's Minutes that you can adapt to the setting. The best source of material is your imagination and that of your fellow Scouts. Television, movies, and the events of the day provide wonderful opportunities for humorous skits and stories. However, if you are in charge, know what each performer will be doing. Check each plan to maintain the highest of Scouting traditions.

BROTHERHOOD MEMBERSHIP

From the beginning of the Order in 1915, all members have been equal. There are no ranks. As an Ordeal member you are entitled to all the rights and privileges of membership in the Order. Yet, so important is the induction sequence that the Order strengthened it by creating Brotherhood membership. It is an opportunity for members to evaluate their unit service since their Ordeal induction.

Brotherhood membership is sought by Arrowmen seeking to reaffirm their belief in the high purposes of the Order. Before becoming a Brotherhood member, each Arrowman makes a special effort to serve his troop or team. Each Brotherhood member commits to even more service to Scouting through the Order.

Completing your Ordeal set you on the next part of your "long and toilsome journey," applying what you learned in your Ordeal to your life. When you have learned about the ideals of the Order and made them a part of your life, you may become a Brotherhood member. Becoming a Brotherhood member marks the completion of your induction into the Order of the Arrow.

Except for making the necessary arrangements for Brotherhood ceremonies, it is not necessary for Brotherhood members to meet as a separate group. Social and service activities are not held for Brotherhood members apart from other members of the lodge.

The Ordeal, with its tests and ceremonies, presents many ideas and ideals. During the months that follow, you think about your Ordeal. Practicing the principles taught in the Ordeal deepens your understanding of them. Each new experience strengthens your commitment to the Order's principles and purposes. Finally, you are able to accept the additional obligations and insights of the Brotherhood.

Your sole obligation as an Ordeal member is to serve your troop or team, and only after you are satisfied that you are doing this are you ready for more. The Brotherhood obligation includes a pledge to support the work of the Order. As an Ordeal member, you are welcome to participate in lodge activities, but you have no obligation to do so. As you approach Brotherhood membership, you should develop a definite idea of how you can serve the Order.

Your Ordeal consisted primarily of physical impressions. The Brotherhood ceremony is one of deeper and quieter mental impressions.

To prepare yourself for Brotherhood membership, refer to the section titled "On the Trail to Brotherhood," immediately following the explanation of the Vigil Honor.

VIGIL HONOR

Alertness to the needs of others is the mark of the Vigil Honor. It calls for an individual with an unusual awareness of the possibilities within each situation.

The Vigil Honor is a high mark of distinction and recognition reserved for those Arrowmen who, by reason of exceptional service, personal effort, and unselfish interest, have made distinguished contributions beyond the immediate responsibilities of their position or office to one or more of the following: their lodge, the Order of the Arrow, Scouting, or their Scout camp. Under no circumstances should tenure in Scouting or the Order of the Arrow be considered as reason enough for a Vigil Honor recommendation.

The Vigil Honor is the highest honor that the Order of the Arrow can bestow upon its members for service to lodge, council, and Scouting. It dates from the year 1915, when founder E. Urner Goodman became the first Vigil Honor member. Since then, thousands of members have been given this honor.

Vigil Honor members have an honorable tradition to uphold. They must at all times conduct themselves in accordance with the ideals of Scouting, the Order of the Arrow, and the Vigil Honor. Membership cannot be won by a person's conscious endeavor. It comes as a recognition of unselfish leadership in service. This fact should be given careful consideration in the selection of candidates for membership. The Vigil Honor has successfully fulfilled a definite and satisfactory service to the Order of the Arrow, to Scouting, and to individual members. Its continued success depends on the care with which future members are selected and on the maintenance by its members of the high ideals of service to others for which the Vigil Honor has always been known.

Any member of the Order of the Arrow registered in Scouting and in good standing in a regularly chartered lodge is eligible for recommendation to the national Order of the Arrow committee for elevation to the Vigil Honor, provided that, at the time of the recommendation, the individual has been a Brotherhood member for a minimum of two years. Because the Order of the Arrow is primarily an organization for youth, it is suggested that, in recommending candidates for the Vigil Honor, preference be given to those who became members of the Order as Scouts rather than to those who were inducted into the Order as adult volunteers or professional Scouters.

Members of the Order can be inducted into the Vigil Honor only with the written approval of the national Order of the Arrow committee.

ON THE TRAIL TO BROTHERHOOD

Your completion of the Ordeal sets you on the path of an exciting adventure. After at least 10 months of active service to your unit, you will be eligible to seal your membership in the Brotherhood ceremony.

The Ordeal has introduced you to the mysteries of the Order. Now, during the service to your unit as an Ordeal member, you have ample opportunity to increase your knowledge of the Arrow and to make it work for you.

This handbook provides all the basic information you will need during this important time. Your brothers in the Order stand ready to help also, and you should take advantage of their support whenever possible.

The Challenges of Brotherhood Membership

You must meet five challenges before you can enter the Circle of the Brotherhood:

1. **Memorize the signs of Arrow membership.** Memorize the Obligation of the Order, which you received from Allowat Sakima (printed on the back of your membership card and in this handbook). Also, memorize the Order of the Arrow Official Song, the Admonition, the sign of Ordeal membership, and the Order of the Arrow handclasp.

2. **Advance in your understanding of the Ordeal.** Gain a thorough understanding of the Ordeal through which you have passed. See "The Customs and Traditions of the Ordeal" in this handbook.

3. **Serve your unit.** Maintain your registration in Scouting. During a period of at least 10 months, strive to fulfill your Obligation by continuing and expanding your service to your own troop or team.

4. **Plan for service in your lodge.** Pay your dues in your Order of the Arrow lodge. Be aware that acceptance of Brotherhood membership involves a pledge of future service to the lodge. Develop a concrete idea of how you plan to fulfill this pledge.

5. **Review your progress.** When you earnestly feel that you have met the four challenges above, write a letter to your lodge or chapter secretary (depending on who is administering the induction). In this letter:

   - Explain what you think the Obligation means,

   - Describe how you have been fulfilling this Obligation in your troop or team and in your daily life, and how you have used your understanding of the Ordeal to aid in your service, and

   - Describe your specific plans for giving future service in the lodge program.

   Include with this letter your advance registration application and fees for the next Brotherhood ceremony according to the instructions given by the lodge. Brotherhood membership can only be conferred by an Arrowman's home lodge—the lodge that serves the council in which the Arrowman's unit is chartered.

Your life as a Brotherhood member. Brotherhood members have pledged to serve the Order. This service takes many forms. Your Scout leader encourages you on, speaks well of the lodge, and gets you a ride to Order of the Arrow events. Your Scout leader is serving the Order. Another Scout in your unit gives camp promotion talks in neighboring troops. Still another Brother is training to be an Elangomat at the next Ordeal. Your junior assistant Scoutmaster is unit elections chairman. An assistant Scout leader is a carpenter who takes tools to camp whenever he or she goes to help the camp ranger with odd jobs. All are serving the Order, each in a personal way; each as other commitments permit.

As a Brotherhood member your first responsibility in Scouting is still your troop or team. Your Scout leader relies on your example, as an older, more experienced Scout; on your willingness to teach; on your leadership. Yet as a Brotherhood member you want to take on more responsibilities in the Order. How do you reconcile this with your responsibility to your unit?

Before assuming any new task, discuss it with your Scout leader. Together, determine how it affects your troop or team life. When your Scout leader knows you are working for Scouting outside your unit, he or she can better help you plan your activities within the unit.

Start by limiting yourself to responsibilities that will not conflict with your troop or team. For example, agree to do elections for new members only on nights when your unit doesn't meet. If you eventually choose to assume a leadership role in the Order, recognize that you will have less time to spend with your unit. As a chapter or lodge officer, you will have to plan around the needs of all the Brothers, not just those in your own unit.

As you plan your service to the Order, you will want to do three things. Find ways to get involved. Understand your own needs and desires. Remember, there are many ways to serve in the Order. You will be most successful as a Brotherhood member if you match your service to your needs. Finally, if you have the opportunity, discuss possible service with a lodge or chapter officer, who will cheerfully show you many ways to serve.

The Order of the Arrow is a service organization. It serves Scouting by promoting the Scout Oath and Law and especially the principles of brotherhood, cheerfulness, and service. It serves Scouting by promoting Scout camping and by building and maintaining camping traditions. It serves Scouting by turning your habit of a daily Good Turn into a lifetime purpose of leadership in cheerful service.

The Order is the Brothers who strive to fulfill its Obligation, and you are a Brother. When your example promotes the principles, when your help to a fellow Scout makes that Scout a better camper, when your daily Good Turn becomes a life of leadership in service, when you remember the Admonition, **you are the Order.**

Questions and Answers

Q. Who is Kichkinet? Nutiket? Meteu? Allowat Sakima?

A. Kichkinet is your guide in the ceremonies. He symbolizes leadership. Nutiket is the guard of the Circle. He upholds the tradition of cheerfulness. Meteu is the medicine man and representative of brotherhood. He reminds us of our need to love one another. Allowat Sakima, the mighty chief, symbolizes service. From him you accepted the Obligation of the Order.

Q. What tokens did the four ceremonial characters reveal to you in the pre-Ordeal, and what did they represent?

A. Nutiket gave the bow to Allowat Sakima as a token of liveliness and flexibility under stress, the principle of cheerfulness. Meteu gave the bowstring to Allowat Sakima as a token of the ties of Brotherhood also symbolized by the rope in the Ordeal ceremony. Allowat Sakima strung the bow uniting brotherhood and cheerfulness for service, and drew an arrow from a quiver as a token that your election separated you from your fellows for something higher. Allowat Sakima asked you to test the bow as a sign of willingness to test the dedication to Scout ideals which led to your election. Lastly, Kichkinet shot the arrow upward, symbolizing the pathway you will follow if your dedication is unwavering.

Q. What are the tests of the Ordeal, and what do they illustrate?

A. The night alone focuses attention on your need for courage and self-reliance on the trail ahead. You must be willing to accept individual responsibility for your thoughts and actions. You will find that your course will set you apart from your friends to the extent of isolation, but you must act according to your resolution regardless of what others do or fail to do.

Your pledge of silence emphasizes the continuing need for you to spend time in thoughtful silence. Difficult decisions will face you now and in the future, and you will need to search your heart and spirit deeply to find the resolution that will guide you onward successfully.

The scant food test illustrates self-denial. Often you will find it necessary to abandon mere personal comfort or desires if you are to fulfill your Obligation.

The day of work indicates your willingness to give service, even when this service involves hardship and toil. In the Ordeal, you worked with the help and cooperation of other candidates and members, but now you must be ready to serve without the help and cooperation of others.

Q. What are the three symbolic preparations for the Obligation?

A. Before you entered the circle, you placed your hand on the shoulder of the candidate ahead of you to indicate your intention to continue in service to your own Scout unit. Kichkinet, seeing that you all had the same purpose, symbolized this bond of brotherhood by binding you all together with the rope. Finally, upon Allowat Sakima's direction, Kichkinet asked you to advance before the fire of cheerfulness.

Q. What is the tradition given us by Uncas as described in the legend?

A. The legend tells how the peaceful lives of the Lenni Lenape Indians were threatened by neighboring tribes and distant enemies. Chief Chingachgook's call for volunteers to go and alert other villages of the tribe was met with apathy and indifference from tribal members. Uncas cheerfully offered his help despite the negative attitudes of everyone around him. He cared enough for others that he was willing to face hardship and danger to protect them from harm. Uncas clearly saw a higher vision, and his desire for his brothers was that they could see it, too. The self-sacrificing service given by Uncas and Chingachgook is said to have saved the tribe from annihilation.

Q. What is the significance of Allowat Sakima's description of the Arrow in the Ordeal ceremony?

A. Allowat Sakima stated that the various qualities attributed to the Arrow are ingredients of leadership. This is a continuation of his comments about the Arrow in the pre-Ordeal. The Ordeal asks individuals to act according to their highest sense of right, regardless of the attitudes or actions of others. The four tests and the Obligation point the way, and Allowat Sakima reveals this way as one of real leadership. Any member who understands his or her Obligation and is striving to fulfill it becomes a center of strength in his or her troop. His or her example sets the pace in cheerful service, and his or her dedication has a rich effect on those who know him or her. Although wearing the sash identifies a Scout or Scouter as a member of the Order, it is his or her efforts to fulfill his or her Obligation that truly distinguishes him or her and provides others with glimpses of the Arrow.

Q. What is Ordeal membership?

A. Like the Ordeal, it is a time of trial, during which your understanding of the traditions of the Arrow will be put to the test. In the Ordeal ceremony, each advancement you made into the circle was challenged, but your resolution and faithfulness in time of testing enabled you to go forward. You will find this to be true also in the experiences ahead. By striving to fulfill your Obligation, you will provide the higher vision of Brotherhood, Cheerfulness, and Service to your fellow Scouts, even as Uncas did for his tribe.

Q. When are you ready to accept Brotherhood membership in the Order?

A. Successfully meeting the demands of the Obligation is usually rather hard for the first several months. Gradually, however, your dedication to it will bring about changes that will make it easier for you. Eventually, the Spirit of Cheerful Service will become almost second nature to you, and you will be fulfilling the Obligation and hardly even thinking about it. As this experience develops, you are beginning to see the Arrow, and you are ready for the Brotherhood.

FUTURE SERVICE FOR ARROWMEN

In addition to service, fellowship, and fun during the years of membership in the Order of the Arrow, there are many opportunities for service that Arrowmen can look forward to in the future. The lessons learned in Scouting and in the Order are of great value in preparing for positions of leadership in tomorrow's world. Cheerful service to our fellow men often becomes a lifelong habit. As members of the lodge mature and take their places in adult society, they will find the following ways to continue their interests in Scouting and service.

Alpha Phi Omega. This is a national service fraternity for college and university students, founded in 1925 and now active on more than 450 campuses in the United States. Its purpose is to assemble college students in the fellowship of the principles of the Boy Scouts of America as embodied in its Scout Oath and Law, to develop leadership; to promote friendship; to provide service to humanity; and to further the freedom that is our national, educational, and intellectual heritage.

Arrowmen interested in membership in this fraternity may contact that office for detailed information.

> Alpha Phi Omega National Service Fraternity
> 14901 East 42nd Street
> Independence, MO 64055
> Telephone: 816-373-8667
> E-mail: executive.director@apo.org

The National Eagle Scout Association. Eagle Scouts may join the National Eagle Scout Association. Many local councils have an active committee with a chairman who usually serves on the council executive board. It's a fine way to give active service to Scouting. Contact your council service center for more information.

College Scouter Reserve. Arrowmen unable to continue active unit service while in college may continue their registration with the Boy Scouts of America by joining the College Scouter Reserve. This will permit them to maintain their membership in an Order of the Arrow lodge. Applications are available through the local council service center.

Volunteer leadership in Scouting. The growth of Scouting depends upon capable, dedicated volunteer leadership. Most Arrowmen have the know-how and leadership capabilities needed in Scouting leadership today.

Volunteer leadership positions in Scouting present a challenging opportunity. Councils are continually in need of qualified individuals to serve as unit leaders, unit committee members, commissioners, merit badge counselors, and in other positions in the district and council. Arrowmen serving in any leadership capacity can continue their active membership in an Order of the Arrow lodge.

Volunteer service in Scouting can become a lifelong interest and a fascinating hobby that fulfills one of the highest callings of good citizenship. A great many of the Cubmasters, Scoutmasters, Varsity team Coaches, Venture crew Advisors, and their associates who will lead units are now active members of the Order of the Arrow.

"He alone is worthy to wear the arrow who will continue faithfully to serve his fellow man."

Professional Scouting. Arrowmen who have a definite desire to serve others should consider professional Scouting as a career.

Scouting is the largest voluntary youth organization in the free world. As Scouting continues to grow, there is an opportunity each year for more than 500 individuals to join its professional ranks.

Your Scout executive or a member of the council professional staff will be glad to talk with you about career opportunities with the Boy Scouts of America. Arrowmen seriously considering professional Scouting should continue unit service and their membership in the Order of the Arrow during college.

UNIFORM AND INSIGNIA

The official insignia of the Order of the Arrow are some of the most colorful in Scouting. It is the responsibility of all Arrowmen to wear them proudly and correctly.

Only currently registered members of the Boy Scouts of America and the Order may wear the insignia of the Order of the Arrow.

An explanation of the various insignia is included below.

Arrow sashes. The official Order of the Arrow sash is available for members through the lodge or local council service center, or through the Supply Group of the Boy Scouts of America. It is a white fabric sash with a red arrow embroidered upon it.

Ordeal members wear the sash with a red embroidered arrow. Brotherhood members wear the sash with a red embroidered arrow enclosed by two red bars.

Vigil Honor members alone wear the sash with a red embroidered arrow enclosed between two red bars, bearing a red triangle superimposed on the arrow shaft. Within the red triangle are three white arrows.

The Order of the Arrow sash is worn with the official Scout field uniform or Scouting's official adult dress wear (a blue blazer and gray slacks). The sash also may be worn by Elangomats who are not in uniform at an Ordeal, youth wearing ceremonial attire, and in such other instances as approved by the Scout executive. The sash is worn over the right shoulder so that the arrow is pointing over the right shoulder. The sash is worn diagonally across the chest. It is not to be worn in any other manner.

Sashes may not be altered in any way or form. Beading or any other material is not permitted on the sash. Nothing is to be worn on the sash, including signatures, patches of any kind, pins, or legends. The only exceptions are the 50th and 60th anniversary awards. Either of these may be worn as an option, by those who have earned them, on the shoulder portion above the bar at the point of the arrow.

The sash is worn at Order of the Arrow functions and special Scouting activities, when members need to be identified as Arrowmen rendering special services.

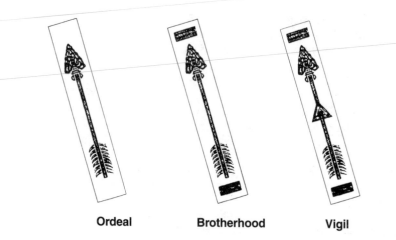

Ordeal   **Brotherhood**   **Vigil**

Lodge pocket flap. Cloth lodge emblems ("flaps") are made available by most lodges. National policy requires that these pocket flap patches be made of, and embroidered on, cloth, and must be of a size and shape so as to cover the right breast pocket flap and not extend beyond the outer edge of the uniform pocket flap. They usually show the lodge name and totem. All OA patches must include "BSA" or the Boy Scout emblem in their patch designs. Chapter or clan flaps are not permitted. There will be no honor distinction denoted by the flap or flap border.

Beading of flaps is against uniform and insignia policy. The national Order of the Arrow committee recommends that no restrictions be placed on the purchase of lodge flap patches. *Members may only wear the lodge pocket flap of the lodge where their dues are paid.*

If the lodge has been recognized with one of the levels of achievement in the lodge Journey to Excellence program, members of the lodge may wear a JTE pin on their lodge flap. *Only the most recent pin awarded may be worn,* and it must be mounted against the left vertical border of the flap.

Universal Arrow Ribbon

Universal Arrow ribbon signifying membership. This is a silver arrow suspended from a red-and-white ribbon. It is worn hanging from the button of the right breast pocket of the uniform shirt. It is to be worn only with the official Scout uniform.

Vigil Honor Pin

Founder's Award Arrow ribbon. Recipients of the Founder's Award are entitled to wear the Founder's Award Arrow ribbon, which is similar to the Universal Arrow ribbon, except that it is a gold-colored arrow suspended from a red ribbon.

Vigil Honor pin. The Vigil Honor pin is worn by Vigil Honor members only, on nonuniform attire or centered on the red and white Universal Arrow ribbon.

Distinguished Service Award Square Knot

Distinguished Service Award square knot. An embroidered cloth knot (white knot on red cloth) is available for holders of the Order's National Distinguished Service Award. The knot is worn as prescribed in the BSA *Insignia Guide.*

Distinguished Service Award Lapel Pin

Distinguished Service Award lapel pin. This pin is for nonuniform wear. Only Arrowmen who have been awarded the DSA may wear this silver lapel pin.

Civilian Arrow pin. The Arrow pin is for nonuniform wear. This simple silver lapel pin may be worn by all members of the Order.

Adviser's badge of office. A special adviser's patch is available for currently appointed section, lodge, and chapter advisers. The associate adviser is an optional position that, with proper prior approval, may be appointed to help fulfill the mission of the lodge. The patch is to be worn on the left sleeve of the uniform in the location prescribed for the badge of office. These badges of office are the only badges authorized for Order of the Arrow adviser positions.

Troop or team representative's badge of office. A special patch is available for youth members (under age 18) appointed to the position of OA troop or team representative. The patch is to be worn on the left sleeve of the uniform in the location prescribed for the badge of office. These are the only badges of office authorized for Order of the Arrow youth positions.

Patch collecting. Patch collecting and trading is as old as Scouting. Millions of Scouts have found patch trading a unique hobby, equally as exciting as collecting stamps or coins are to philatelists and numismatists.

Principles of fair play must always dominate every patch trading experience. Money must never be exchanged as part of patch trading. No high-pressure tactics should ever be involved. You may find that Order of the Arrow events have specifically scheduled hours, times, or locations for patch trading. You should conform to these standards. The BSA regulation regarding badge swapping is as follows (from the *Insignia Guide*):

"Boy Scouts and Venturers attending jamborees may swap among themselves articles and novelties of a local or regional nature. The swapping of such items as badges of office, rank, distinguished service, training, performance, achievement, and distinction, however, is a violation of Article X of the *Rules and Regulations of the Boy Scouts of America,* forbidding the holding of these badges by any but the members who have complied with the requirements for them."

THE SCOUTER'S ROLE

The role of the adult Scouter in the Order of the Arrow is the same as it is throughout Scouting. Scouters help young people grow through a program the youth plan and run. This help includes training, counseling, and advising leaders and sometimes counseling individual members.

There are, however, some practical differences. In the troop or team, there are fewer adult leaders than boy leaders, so each Scouter is kept busy advising several Scouts. On the other hand, at Order of the Arrow events there are far more Scouters present than elected lodge leaders. Thus, most Scouters in the Order must take a back-seat role, lending support for those who attend Order functions, but without a direct advisory relationship to any leader.

As a Scouter, you wear the Arrow to make it more significant to Scouts. If you were elected as an adult, it was for this reason, rather than as an honor or award. Nonetheless, your own induction into the Order is your opportunity for personal growth. Further, you are observed by younger Arrowmen and must be an exemplary participant.

A note of caution: If you were an active Arrowman as a youth, you have the special challenge of learning new leadership styles. No longer will you be planning, voting, leading. Now you have far greater joys as you watch the young men achieve their successes.

There are two distinct Scouter roles in the Order: that of the adviser appointed for a particular youth leader, and that of other Scouters.

Role of the adviser in the Order. Each chapter or lodge officer or committee chairman has an appointed adviser. Officers in the Order are elected by the youth members, and the officers appoint committee chairmen. Advisers are appointed or approved by the Scout executive, usually for the same term as the officers. The Scout executive, as the lodge's Supreme Chief of the Fire, is the highest adviser in the lodge.

Each adviser in the Order provides support for the program to which he or she has been assigned. It is inappropriate for an adviser to run the program, although he or she should always be involved. It is the adviser's task to make sure that the young men succeed. This includes training, transportation, and staying constantly involved and informed.

The proper role of an adviser is the same as the proper role of a Scoutmaster or Varsity team Coach. An adviser works almost completely behind the scenes. Although the Order's program is more complex than that of a troop or team, the leaders in the Order are older and more experienced. Yet, they still benefit from sound guidance and enthusiastic support. Watching outstanding youth leaders succeed is one of the most enjoyable parts of being an adviser.

Role of the nonadviser Scouter. As a Scouter without an adviser appointment, your main responsibility in Scouting lies outside the Order of the Arrow. Your main duty within the Order is to support its program in your Scouting position.

If you serve as Scoutmaster or Coach, you know that your attitudes will be reflected in those of your Scouts. You may not have the time to attend Order activities regularly. Unit functions, roundtables, and Scout leader training come first. But you can make your feelings toward the Order known. Since you understand the importance of your troop or team to the Order, you can speak well of it. As a result your Scouts will support both. Since your time is limited, assign one of your assistants who is an Arrowman a special responsibility to advise your Order of the Arrow troop or team representative. Your Arrowmen will then have a source of transportation and an additional source of inspiration.

Many Scouters find Order of the Arrow functions as an excellent opportunity to relax, take stock, meet other Scouters, and get to know their youth leaders better. Your efforts to support the Arrow during these activities will be appreciated. Offer transportation or help with a special skill. But especially give your positive example and encouragement to all Brothers.

AMERICAN INDIAN CUSTOMS AND TRADITIONS

A fascinating feature of the Order of the Arrow is its wide use of American Indian lore, customs, and attire. Many people are interested in the history, traditions, and customs of American Indians. This study, as a by-product of the program, has become a popular hobby for many youth and adults who first became aware of Indian lore through their Order of the Arrow membership.

Your first exposure to this was probably in viewing the ceremonial team, with its four principal characters: Allowat Sakima, the mighty chief; Meteu, the medicine man; Nutiket, the guard; Kichkinet, the guide. While Indian traditions are used for dramatic effect in the ceremonies and terminology of the Order, under no circumstances should emphasis be placed upon the Indian aspects of the program to the degree that they obscure the purpose of the Order of the Arrow. As such, a dance team is not the most important or necessary part of the Order's organization.

Pronunciation of key words. Here is a simple guide to help you with pronunciation of Indian words you will often hear.

In the Legend

The Delaware Indians	Lenni Lenape	leh-NEE len-AH-pay
The Chieftain	Chingachgook	CHING-GOTCH-gook
The Chieftain's son	Uncas	UN-cuss

The Principles and Full Name of the Order

Brotherhood	Wimachtendienk	wee-MOK-TEN-dee-enk
Cheerfulness	Wingolauchsik	WIN-go-louch-sik
Service	Witahemui	WIT-ah-HEM-oo-ee

The Ceremonial Characters

The Mighty Chief	Allowat Sakima	AH-lo-wot sah-KEE-ma
The Medicine Man	Meteu	meh-TAY-oh
The Guard	Nutiket	noo-TEE-ket
The Guide	Kichkinet	KITCH-kin-et

Initial understanding. Each American Indian tribe is different. Hollywood portrays Indians as wearing feathered headdresses and beadwork patterns, living in tepees, and riding horses. Yet many tribes never practiced these customs. Some of these customs did not exist until introduced by Europeans. Many aspects of the plains Indian cultures did not exist before the arrival of the horse with the Spanish. What we call American Indian beadwork is made of manufactured glass beads, as were traded to American Indians by Europeans. Handmade beads were not worn in large patterns on clothing because of the work it took to make each bead. Still, beadwork is a genuine American Indian craft.

Know the historical and geographical context of a particular practice. American Indian cultures were not static even before European settlement, and changed after European contact. Even before the 1500s, lifestyles differed markedly across the hemisphere. Tribes separated by only several hundred miles had very different lifestyles. Without such understanding, your attempts to honor and spread knowledge of Indian culture may do exactly the opposite.

Specialize to gain understanding. A smattering of learning about the various tribes gains you little. Deep study of a single one of the widely differing groups will give you a sincere appreciation of their way of life.

Choose a tribe that does or did live locally, since more material will be available to you. The best place to start is at the library. Use the card catalog to make a list of everything available about the tribe. As you read the cards in the subject catalog, be on alert for tribal names. The name you apply to the tribe may not have been what they called themselves. (It might be a derisive term applied by neighboring enemies.) Thus, one tribe may be given several names, or, even more confusing, the same name may be applied to several groups of people.

Most tribes consisted of those people who spoke the same language. Europeans treated each American Indian tribe as a small cohesive country. Yet some did not have strong political structures above the village level. Even social structures, such as annual events, varied somewhat from group to group within a single people.

Reading and research. Use your list to start with the books that will be best for you. There are three distinct kinds of literature on American Indian lore. First, there are popularizations such as the books by Ben Hunt. These are valuable for getting people interested in American Indian culture, and may contain some practical material on American Indian crafts. But the details are often not authentic. If the author does not give the tribe, geographical location, and historical era, consider it suspect.

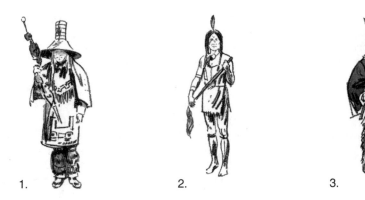

1.

2.

3.

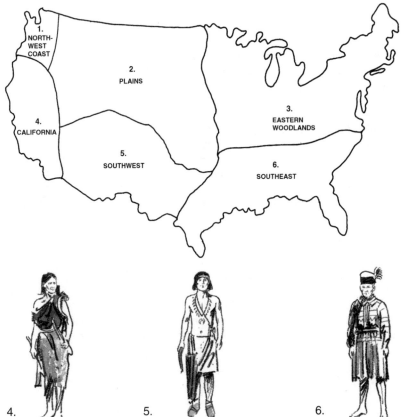

1.
NORTH-
WEST
COAST

2.
PLAINS

3.
EASTERN
WOODLANDS

4.
CALIFORNIA

5.
SOUTHWEST

6.
SOUTHEAST

4.

5.

6.

Second, there are scholarly works that are archaeological (studies of the past by traces left in the soil), historical (written records of early contacts), or anthropological (studies of culture by observation and interview). The primary works—those which report the original research—are scientific journals, scholarly reports, and monographs. Many of these were sponsored and printed by the U.S. government. Scholars summarize the primary sources and rework the data into surveys and textbooks. Textbooks introduce the subject to a newcomer, while surveys usually tour some part of the entire field for the specialist. Look for textbooks and introductory surveys. The reference librarian at your school, public, or local college library can be most helpful. Even if the book is not available locally, your librarian can often obtain it for you through sharing arrangements with other libraries.

Finally, there are books and periodicals about modern American Indian culture. This includes material on ceremonies, dancing, and crafts as they are done today. Much of this material is not about any particular Indian group, but focuses on the major reservations in the western United States.

Using local American Indian traditions. Lodges are encouraged to study the customs of the American Indian tribes that live or lived in the area of their council territory. If possible, a lodge should model its attire after those of the local tribes.

Some lodges have set up committees to gather information from libraries, museums, and ethnologists at local colleges. Many colleges and universities have literature, exhibits, and archives that interested OA members may research for information on authentic American Indian attire, customs, traditions and language.

It is best for each lodge to follow the general attire of the American Indian tribes of its home area. It may require some extra time and effort, plus a bit of detective work, to piece together enough authentic information, but it can be done. Some lodges have adopted a broader pattern for traditions and attire, such as those worn by the Plains Indians or another large regional group near its council area.

American Indian dances. A Scout is reverent. Observing the twelfth point of the Scout Law has two equal parts: Doing your duty to God, and respecting the religious beliefs of others. Scouts must even respect beliefs no longer practiced. Many traditional dances of various American Indian tribes have religious themes.

We must always remember that a religion belongs to the people practicing it. A nonbeliever cannot perform a sacred dance without degrading or insulting the original religious intent. For this reason, any dance that has religious connotations must be avoided.

You would be offended if your worship service was used for entertainment. Doing a religious Indian dance as a nonbeliever is just as offensive. Religion has a strong role in American Indian cuture. Therefore, learn and respect the difference between the social dances, songs, crafts, and regalia, and those associated with religious practices. Care in this regard will help you appreciate the American Indian life all the more.

Your lodge should have members who are sensitive to and informed about this issue. Contact these members, work with them, and heed their advice. Then you can honor rather than debase the culture of the true discoverers of America.

The following general rules will assist in recognizing those dances that should be avoided:

(1) Dances utilizing a mask, including the use of Katchinas, false faces, Northwest Coast masks, and many others. (2) Pipe ceremonies invoking spirits. (3) Petitions to a higher power, including blessings, thanksgiving prayers for rain, food, or a good harvest. The most abused dance of this type is the Hopi snake dance. These dances should be avoided, even though they may be favored by young dancers who judge the merits of a dance only by the action opportunities it presents.

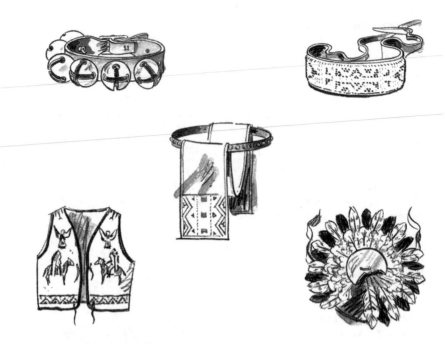

American Indian attire materials. Many materials for making attire are available to anyone willing to look for them. There are suppliers of American Indian crafts in most parts of our country. Check current issues of *Whispering Wind* and *Boys' Life* magazines for the listings.

Try to get as close to the original material as is economically and legally possible. There are many fine substitutes that are usable, although some leather substitutes are more expensive than leather itself. An old navy blue blanket or trade cloth can be used, but should be dry-cleaned and not allowed to get wet. When making cloth leggings, make them in the cloth style. Never use cloth as imitation leather.

Feathers also can be a problem. Your safest bet is imitation eagle feathers made from turkey feathers. Many state and federal laws protect endangered birds. Both our native eagles are under the protection of federal laws that prohibit the possession or transfer of eagle feathers from bald eagles killed after June 8, 1940, and from golden eagles killed after October 24, 1962. The law covers all methods of getting new eagle feathers, so stick to the best imitations or substitutions you can get.

Resource material on American Indian lore. There are literally hundreds of books describing the traditions and customs, attire, and ceremonial regalia of the American Indians in every part of our country. Some of these books are listed in the bibliography of this handbook.

The bibliography lists more than 100 books, pamphlets, and periodicals about American Indians. These references offer a handy resource for Arrowmen who would like to learn more about the history and culture of the various tribes that first inhabited these lands. Your experience as an Arrowman could lead to a solid background and lifelong interest in this subject.

The bibliography is organized geographically so that you can read about the American Indians of your particular area. There also are lists pertaining to American Indian attire, crafts, and dances. Following the bibliography is a Lenni Lenape word list that provides a fairly extensive vocabulary for this dialect.

The reference materials may be found at your school or public library; ask the librarian for other books about American Indians. Go to any museums in your community that contain Indian exhibits, and visit the websites of national museums and associations. One good resource is the National Museum of the American Indian, at http://www.nmai.si.edu.

Structure, Program, and Awards

The Order of the Arrow is fully integrated with the outdoor program of the Boy Scouts of America as Scouting's National Honor Society.

Nationally, the magnitude and dynamics of the Order of the Arrow program require administration by a full-time paid staff. This staff works at the national office and is responsible for carrying out all aspects of the Order's program, including: national conferences; involvement in national programs such as jamborees; producing all OA publications, including this handbook, ceremonial pamphlets, and the *National Bulletin;* Vigil Honor and Founder's Award recognitions; lodge charter renewal; liaison with local councils; and conducting all business and financial matters of the Order nationally.

The staff is headed by the director of the Order of the Arrow. He is assisted by an OA specialist.

The Order is a self-funded program and pays all costs associated with its operation through its own revenue sources, which include annual lodge charter fees and recognition sales.

Correspondence to the national committee should be forwarded to:

Order of the Arrow, S235

Boy Scouts of America

1325 West Walnut Hill Lane

P.O. Box 152079

Irving, TX 75015-2079

NATIONAL ORDER OF THE ARROW COMMITTEE

The national Order of the Arrow committee, a support committee of the national Outdoor Adventures Committee, sets policy and directs the program of the Order. The Order has more than 171,000 members nationally, organized into 300 lodges, grouped into sections of the four regions.

The volunteer leader is the chairman of the national Order of the Arrow committee. The chairman is appointed annually by the chairman of the national Outdoor Adventures Committee. Members of the national Order of the Arrow committee are appointed annually by their chairman.

The staff advisers to the national committee are the director of the Order of the Arrow and the OA specialist. These individuals are national professional Scouters. The national chief, national vice chief, immediate past chief, and immediate past vice chief serve as youth members on the national committee along with approximately 50 other Arrowmen.

To implement and manage the program of the Order of the Arrow, the national committee is organized as follows:

- Communications and Technology

- Development

- Financial Operations and Strategic Planning

- National Events and 100th Anniversary

- Outdoor Adventures

- Recognition, Awards, History, and Preservation

- Region and Section Operations

- Training

- Unit, Chapter, and Lodge Support

Vice chairmen of the national committee are appointed by the chairman annually to manage and administer each of these areas.

Every five years the national committee establishes a Strategic Planning Task Force. Organized across functional areas, the task force develops the Order's five-year plan for growth and improvement.

Because of the size and complexity of the program and the number of individuals who serve on the committee to deliver the program across the country, a steering committee has been created to manage the day-to-day affairs of the program. As a whole, the national committee meets semiannually; the steering committee meets two additional times during the year. Various members of the steering committee are in constant contact with one another to handle affairs of the Order on a daily basis. Members of the steering committee are the national chairman, national vice chairmen, past national chairmen, national chief, and national vice chief. The director of the Order of the Arrow and the OA specialist serve as nonvoting members.

NATIONAL ORDER OF THE ARROW CONFERENCE (NOAC)

Every two years, during the month of August, the Order of the Arrow holds a national conference on the campus of a major university. The national conference is held over six days with from 6,000 to 7,000 Arrowmen usually participating, coming from throughout the United States and its territories, and some from overseas. The conference program includes innovative leadership development programs, fellowship periods, inspirational gatherings (shows), ceremony team development, American Indian pageants, camping promotion, and opportunities to hear and talk with national leaders of the Order of the Arrow and the Boy Scouts of America.

PHILMONT ORDER OF THE ARROW TRAIL CREW

As part of the Order's 1995 Year of Service project, the national Order of the Arrow committee launched a new partnership with the BSA High Adventure Committee. The national Order of the Arrow committee wanted to provide a platform for lodges to strengthen their association with their local council, to further the Order's purpose in providing service, and to support the BSA's outdoor program.

The national Order of the Arrow committee provided financial support for renovation of program areas at Philmont, while logistical help came from the High Adventure Committee. The two joined forces and began what was to have been a one-year, hands-on service project for trail building at the place many consider the summit of Scouting.

Outstanding young Arrowmen from throughout the nation united at Philmont for a two-week period of service, inspiration, team building, and personal development. They revitalized their commitment to Scouting and the principles of the Order of the Arrow.

NORTHERN TIER WILDERNESS VOYAGE

Building on the success of the Philmont Trail Crew and furthering its commitment to BSA high-adventure bases, the national Order of the Arrow committee has launched a similar program at the Charles L. Sommers High Adventure Base in Ely, Minnesota. Begun in 1999, this 13-day experience is divided into two parts. The first half of the voyage focuses on portage trail and campsite maintenance within the Boundary Waters Canoe Area Wilderness on the U.S.–Canadian border; the remaining expedition is spent on a canoeing adventure that is planned and chosen by the participants in the program.

Like the Philmont Trail Crew experience, outstanding Arrowmen from throughout the country strengthen their leadership skills, learn advanced wilderness and no-trace camping skills, learn wilderness safety techniques, participate in many motivational activities, and receive special Order of the Arrow coaching. The Northern Tier Wilderness Voyage is ultimately a journey that challenges Scouts mentally, physically, and spiritually. Participants are expected to use their experience to benefit their troop or team, chapter, lodge, and council programs.

OA OCEAN ADVENTURE

In 2005, the Order of the Arrow launched its third national high-adventure service program, the OA Ocean Adventure (OAOA). Located at the Florida National High Adventure Sea Base in Islamorada, Florida, OAOA is a two-week journey divided into two parts. The first part focuses on PADI scuba diving certification and advancing the individual Arrowman's self-confidence and leadership; the second part is spent fulfilling underwater and land-based conservation projects to help protect the wilderness environment of the beautiful Florida Keys. Throughout the program, emphasis on service, leadership, and the individual Arrowman's responsibility to his unit and lodge is maintained.

Exceptional Arrowmen travel from across the country to build on their foundation of leadership, knowledge, and teamwork through the many opportunities and challenges of the OAOA. Participants will expand their knowledge of marine wildlife habitats and conservation and will gain a new understanding and reaffirmation of the principles of the Order.

NATIONAL CONFERENCE COMMITTEE

The national Order of the Arrow conference is planned and conducted by the national conference committee, which is composed of those youth from across the nation younger than 21 who are currently serving as section chiefs. Section chiefs participate in a national planning meeting held in late December of the year preceding the national conference.

As their first order of business, the section chiefs elect a national chief, national vice chief, and four region chiefs.

To be eligible to hold a national office as national chief, national vice chief, or region chief, a section chief must be younger than 21 during the entire term of office. No person who has ever held one of these national offices can ever again be eligible to hold any national OA office.

These officers serve until their successors are elected at the next planning meeting. The national chief and vice chief organize subcommittees and direct the program planning for the national conference. Members of the national Order of the Arrow committee serve as advisers.

Following the elections, the national conference committee is divided into functional subcommittees, called conference committees, with each section chief being assigned to one after indicating the committee of his preference. The committees meet, and each elects a chairman, called a conference vice chief. Like the section conclave, these committees often include training, special events, ceremonies, shows, competitions and recreation, Founder's Day, camping, American Indian events, and others.

While the responsibilities are definite, it must be remembered that at each level of the Order of the Arrow, the three types of leaders—youth, volunteer, and professional—must work in close harmony to ensure an effective program.

NATIONAL YOUTH OFFICERS

The national Order of the Arrow committee expanded the involvement of youth in the administration of national programs in 1950, when the position of national conference chief was created. At that time, the youth elected to this post was responsible for working with the committee that planned and conducted the national conference. This youth presided over the conference itself, and oversaw committees responsible for planning and conducting its shows, training, etc.

In 1964, when it became apparent that the scope and workload of the national conference chief had expanded beyond those which one person could reasonably handle, and in an effort to enable a second youth to serve in a national leadership role, the position of national conference vice chief was created.

By 1971, the role of the top youth leaders of the conference had expanded to become a year-round role as youth leaders of the Order itself. To reflect this change in roles, the positions of national chief and national vice chief were created, superceding the previous conference positions. At the end of 1974, region chiefs were elected to provide youth leadership in the six BSA regions. Following a BSA realignment, the number of region chiefs was reduced to four at the end of 1992.

The national chief and national vice chief serve as the top youth leaders of the Order, responsible not only for the national conference, but also serving on the national committee to provide youth input in decisions affecting the program nationally.

NATIONAL ORDER OF THE ARROW
PROGRAMS OF EMPHASIS

Year	Event	Location/Theme	Delegates
1948	NOAC	**Indiana University**	1,000
1950	NOAC	**Indiana University**	1,000
1952	NOAC	**Miami University (Ohio)**	2,200
1954	NOAC	**University of Wyoming** *The OA Strengthens the Unit and Council Camping Programs*	1,300
1956	NOAC	**Indiana University** *Service for God and Country*	2,201
1958	NOAC	**University of Kansas** *Brothers in Service, Leaders in Camping*	2,368
1961	NOAC	**Indiana University** *Weld Tightly Every Link*	2,800
1963	NOAC	**University of Illinois** *Catch the Higher Vision*	3,105
1965	NOAC	**Indiana University** *Mindful of Our Traditions*	4,200
1967	NOAC	**University of Nebraska** *With Hearts and Wills United*	4,158
1969	NOAC	**Indiana University** *Pathways to Service*	4,421
1971	NOAC	**University of Illinois** *Aim High, Serve All*	5,200
1973	NOAC	**University of California—Santa Barbara** *New Horizons in Service*	4,400
1975	NOAC	**Miami University (Ohio)** *Foundations for the Future*	4,200
1977	NOAC	**University of Tennessee** *A Thing of the Spirit*	3,900
1979	NOAC	**Colorado State University** *See the Need, Meet the Challenge*	4,351
1981	NOAC	**University of Texas** *First a Spark, Now a Flame*	3,200
1983	NOAC	**Rutgers University** *Those Who Chose You Need You*	3,328
1985	Trek	**Philmont Scout Ranch** *Ponder That Which Is Our Purpose*	1,182
1986	NOAC	**Central Michigan University** *Kindle the Flame From Within*	3,700
1987	Pow Wow	**Northwest Community College—Powell, Wyoming**	500
1988	NOAC	**Colorado State University** *Inspired to Lead, Dedicated to Serve*	4,100
1989	Trek	**Philmont Scout Ranch** *These High Places Are Within You*	880
1990	NOAC	**Indiana University** *Seek the Knowledge, Share the Spirit*	6,900

Year	Event	Location/Theme	Delegates
1991	Task Forces	**Focus '91** *Year of the Lodge*	N/A
1992	NOAC	**University of Tennessee** *Many Fires, One Great Light*	6,800
1993	Jamboree Service	**Fort A. P. Hill, Virginia** OA Service Corps, American Indian Village, Model Campsite	222
1994	NOAC	**Purdue University** *A Journey for One, An Adventure for Many*	6,012
1995	Retreat	**Philmont Training Center** *Year of Service*	400
1996	NOAC	**Indiana University** *See the Dream, Live the Adventure*	6,265
1997	Jamboree Service	**Fort A. P. Hill, Virginia** OA Service Corps, American Indian Village, TOAP, *Odyssey of the Law*	413
1998	NOAC	**Iowa State University** *Memories of the Past, A Vision for the Future*	7,043
1999	Leadership Summit	**Colorado State University** *Supporting Scouting in the 21st Century*	1,127
2000	NOAC	**University of Tennessee** *Bound in Brotherhood, Led by the Spirit*	6,632
2001	Jamboree Service	**Fort A. P. Hill, Virginia** OA Service Corps, American Indian Village, TOAP, *Scoutopia*	461
2002	NOAC	**Indiana University** *Test Yourself, and So Discover*	6,939
2003	Indian Summer	**Ridgecrest Conference Center—Asheville, North Carolina**	908
2004	NOAC	**Iowa State University** *Chosen to Serve, Inspired to Lead*	6,504
2005	Jamboree Service	**Fort A. P. Hill, Virginia** OA Service Corps, American Indian Village, TOAP, *Twelve Cubed*	453
2006	NOAC	**Michigan State University** *The Legend Lives On*	8,003
2007	NCLS	**Indiana University** *Building the Path to Servant Leadership*	1,292
2008	*ArrowCorps[5]*	**USDA Forest Service sites in CA, MO, UT, VA, WY** *A Higher Adventure*	3,674
2009	NOAC	**Indiana University** *The Power of One*	6,803
2010	Jamboree Service	**Fort A.P. Hill, Virginia** OA Service Corps, American Indian Village, *Mysterium Compass*	529
2011	*SummitCorps*	**New River Gorge National River, West Virginia**	1,404
2011	Indian Summer	**Ridgecrest Conference Center, Asheville, North Carolina**	902
2012	NOAC	**Michigan State University** *United, We Leave a Legacy*	7,153

NATIONAL CHIEFS AND VICE CHIEFS

Year	Conference Chief	Conference Vice Chief
1950	J. Richard Wilson	
1952	James R. Montgomery	
1954	James R. Feil	
1956	James L. Waters	
1958	James W. Kolka	
1961	Ronald J. Temple	
1963	Robert B. Ellsperman	Gerald R. McNellis
1965	Michael S. Costello	Earl C. Davis
1967	Robert F. Szczys	Mark R. Samios
1969	Thomas E. Fielder	Philip L. Chabot Jr.

Year	National Chief	National Vice Chief
1971	Paul L. Pruitt	James T. Widmaier
1973	Clifford D. Harmon	Greg A. Guy
1975	Bradley E. Haddock	Edward J. Stumler
1977	Christopher H. Boswell	William "Rick" Burton
1979	Jeffrie A. Herrmann	Lawrence F. Brown Jr.
1981	Bradley D. Starr	Kevin P. Moll
1983	Robert A. Wade	William B. O'Tuel
1985	Stephen D. Mimnaugh	Michael G. Hoffman
1986	David A. Erb	Cary L. Roberts
1988	Jeffery C. Moser	Angelo A. Cappelli
1989	W. Jack Stephens Jr.	Wade A. Herbranson
1990	John E. Meckley III	N. Anthony Steinhardt III
1991	Clint E. Takeshita	Jeffrey L. Posey
1992	Sean J. Cox	H. Blair Dickens
1993	Brian M. Beaverstock	Dameon C. Hutto
1994	Scott W. Beckett	Kyle E. Tanner
1995	Joshua M. Feigelson	David M. Clark
1996	Ryan J. Pitts	Ryan R. Miske
1997	Christopher T. Rogers	Joshua R. Sain
1998	Mathew B. Milleson	David M. Petrush
1999	William G. Parker	Andrew S. Oh
2000	Carey J. Mignerey	Jordan A. Hitchens
2001	Donald J. Cunningham	Scott L. Hunter
2002	Clayton T. Capp	Riley C. Berg
2003	Nicholas P. Digirolamo	Richard J. Moore
2004	Jeffrey E. Hayward	David C. Dowty
2005	Patrick J. Murphy	Seth Y. Mollitt
2006	Sean M. Murray	W. Christopher Schildknecht
2007	Evan P. Chaffee	Larry M. Newton
2008	Jacob P. Wellman	Benjamin L. Stilwill
2009	John J. O'Neill	Daniel J. Higham
2010	Bradford C. Lichota	William G. Swingle
2011	Jonathan D. Hillis	Daniel T. Dick
2012	John P. Rehm	Preston H. Marquis
2013	Matthew E. Brown	Jordan L. Hughes

NATIONAL LEADERSHIP SEMINAR

The National Leadership Seminar is a weekend conference focusing primarily on the skills and attributes of leadership. It is intended primarily to enhance the leadership skills of the Order of the Arrow's key youth and adult members as they seek to improve their service to the Boy Scouts of America and the greater community.

Youth participants should be at least 15 years of age or a lodge officer. Prior completion of the Lodge Leadership Development course is desirable. The seminar is an intensive experience in learning about the nature of leadership and practicing some of the skills that leaders use. While it is designed to be fun, the course is also mentally challenging. Participants should be developmentally, physically, and mentally prepared to actively engage in an exhausting, invigorating weekend.

At the end of the seminar, participants make a contract with themselves to apply the skills learned in the seminar on projects in their unit, lodge, council, and community.

The region sponsors and schedules the seminar, promotes the event, and invites councils to send participants.

NATIONAL LODGE ADVISER TRAINING SEMINAR

The National Lodge Adviser Training Seminar is a weekend conference focusing on the skills and attributes of effective lodge advisers. It is intended primarily to enhance an adviser's knowledge of and connectivity with the Order's strategic plan, program, and resources, while emphasizing the personal skills that are necessary for the development of effective youth leadership and ultimately the lodge deliverance of service to the council program. Among these are effective communications, planning, and counseling.

Participants must be lodge members, age 21 or older, and should be lodge advisers or those with lodge adviser potential, as approved by the Scout executive. Completion of the Lodge Leadership Development Course and the National Leadership Seminar are desirable. The seminar is an intensive experience in learning about the nature of lodge program, delivery of service to the council, and development of the youth leadership necessary to both. While it is designed to be fun, the course is mentally challenging as well. Participants should be open to learning and prepared to actively engage in an invigorating weekend. It is desirable that the lodge adviser and lodge staff adviser attend the same seminar, if possible.

During the seminar, participants develop a series of planned actions. Following the seminar, the planned actions must be reviewed with the Scout executive in a Key 3 meeting. This is termed a "legacy development discussion," since the trained adviser had the greatest chance to leave a legacy of leadership in service. That legacy should include effective mentoring for youth leaders and a strong connectivity to council service needs. Upon completion of the planned actions, the regions will send the seminar recognitions to the council for presentation at a lodge function. At this point, the adviser is also authorized to wear the BSA Trained Leader emblem below the adviser badge of office.

The region organizes and schedules the seminar, promotes the event, and invites councils to send advisers.

REGIONAL ORGANIZATION

The Boy Scouts of America is organized into four geographical regions: Central, Northeast, Southern, and Western.

The region chief is the youth leader of the region elected by the section chiefs from that region at the national planning meeting. He must be younger than 21 during the entire year of his term; he will serve until a successor is elected. The election is held following the election of the national chief and national vice chief.

The volunteer leader in the region is the region Order of the Arrow chairman. Appointed by the chairman of the national Order of the Arrow committee, in coordination with the region director, this person is responsible for administering and managing the program regionally, with a special emphasis placed on the role of adviser to the region chief.

The region staff adviser is appointed by the national General Services Group director. Duties of the region staff adviser include regular communication and counsel with the region OA chairman and region chief.

Each of the regions is divided into geographical areas composed of a number of councils. The number of areas varies according to region. The region director establishes the area boundaries and appoints an area director to provide leadership to the programs within the area. Based on recommendations made by the region Order of the Arrow chairman and region staff adviser, the area director groups councils in each area into one or more sections.

Communication is a very important role for the region. Some regions use a newsletter to keep their sections up-to-date. Each region has a website with its own unique URL:

Central Region: http://www.central.oa-bsa.org

Northeast Region: http://www.northeast.oa-bsa.org

Southern Region: http://www.southern.oa-bsa.org

Western Region: http://www.western.oa-bsa.org

SECTION ORGANIZATION

The section provides an interlodge forum for lodge and chapter leaders, bringing them together for fellowship and mutual improvement through the exchange of ideas. The section organizes and conducts an annual conclave, at which training plays a major part. In addition, the section creates a monitoring/mentoring relationship with their lodges, provides leadership development opportunities, fosters understanding and adherence to national OA policies and procedures, and coordinates OA administrative and program functions.

The section officers are the chief, vice chief, and secretary. They are elected at the annual business meeting held during the conclave. The section adviser is the volunteer leader, and a professional Scouter serves as staff adviser. These Arrowmen are appointed annually by the area director, with the concurrence of the region Order of the Arrow chairman and region staff adviser. The advisers work closely with the section officers in planning and conducting the conclave.

The section adviser is the important link between lodges within the section. This person provides advice and guidance to the section officers and is an important resource of program ideas and help for lodge advisers.

A field operations publication is available for download and printing at the Order's official website, http://www.oa-bsa.org, and should be used by all section officers and advisers. The *Field Operations Guide* is designed as a guide to administration and program pertaining to national, regional, and section operations of the Order. It includes current information about the organizational structure and program, as well as the section rules.

Secondly, the *Field Operations Guide* is dedicated to providing the necessary background, knowledge, and information about how to organize and run a successful section conclave. It is informative and full of helpful hints, including sample training outlines.

Names and addresses of all elected personnel should be sent by the staff adviser to the director of the Order of the Arrow within a week following the election of section officers.

THE ORDER AND INTERNATIONAL SCOUTING

The Order of the Arrow is an integral part of the program of the Boy Scouts of America and operates within its official structure. Neither the Order nor individual members may enter into any type of agreement concerning the Order of the Arrow and another Scout association or individuals in terms of individual or honorary memberships.

Remember, to be eligible for election to the Order, the individual must first be a registered member of the Boy Scouts of America. Recognizing international camp staff participants or members of other national Scout associations with any type of Order of the Arrow membership is contrary to the policies of the Boy Scouts of America. This type of recognition also can create difficulties in the Boy Scouts of America's relationships with other national Scout associations.

SPECIAL PROGRAMS AND AWARDS

A variety of special programs and recognitions have been created by the national Order of the Arrow committee over the years. Each is administered by the director of the Order of the Arrow, and pertinent information and appropriate forms are available for download at www.oa-bsa.org.

Lodge Journey to Excellence program. Having evolved from national Standard Lodge to National Honor Lodge and National Quality Lodge, this program's latest iteration is aligned with the BSA Journey to Excellence. The program evaluates lodge performance and opportunities for continuous improvement. It provides a guide for good lodge administration and recognizes bronze, silver, and gold levels of achievement in program and operation. Similar, complimentary programs have been developed for sections and chapters.

To be considered for one of the three levels of recognition, the lodge must have filed its charter renewal by December 31 with appropriate fees and achieved the necessary point score on the Lodge Journey to Excellence Petition. A copy of the petition is included annually with each lodge's charter renewal and program packets.

The petition's objectives form an overall plan and guide that help ensure a successful lodge program. Achieving at least bronze level of performance is required to apply for all national lodge awards and recognitions.

Josh R. Sain Memorial Scholarships. These college assistance scholarships are awarded annually to immediate past national officers (chief, vice chief, or region chief) and immediate past section chiefs, based on exceptional service and scholarship achievement. The scholarships are given in memory of the 1997 national vice chief, Josh Sain, who died in a car accident during his term of office. The first two awards were given in 1999.

Maury Clancy Indian Campership fund. This campership fund was created in 1971 to help provide funds to those American Indian Scouts needing assistance to attend resident camp. The fund was subsequently named in memory of long-time national committee member Maury Clancy, who contributed significantly to the Order. Mr. Clancy emphasized the significance of our nation's American Indian culture and worked to encourage the preservation of our American Indian heritage. Lodges may contribute to this fund through their section "at will," thereby increasing the fund and enabling more camperships to be awarded.

E. Urner Goodman Camping Award. The award was established as a tribute and testimonial to the Order's founder, E. Urner Goodman. Its purpose is to encourage and challenge Order of the Arrow members and lodges to increase their effectiveness in promoting and increasing Scout camping in each council. Awards are presented to two outstanding lodges in each region annually. For a lodge to be eligible for consideration, the lodge must have achieved at least the bronze level of Journey to Excellence performance, and the E. Urner Goodman Camping Award petition must be completed and forwarded with the lodge's charter renewal application.

National Service Award. The National Service Award was created in 1998 to recognize annually two lodges from each region that have performed outstanding service, both in a qualitative and quantitative manner, for their local council. To be considered for this prestigious award, the lodge must have achieved at least the bronze level of Journey to Excellence performance, and the National Service Award petition must be completed and forwarded with the lodge's charter renewal application.

National Service Grant program. Each year the national Order of the Arrow committee makes available matching grant money to lodges for camp or service center projects in their local councils. The Order will provide up to one-half of the money for a selected service project. The maximum amount that will be granted is $5,000. Selected projects must be consistent with the lodge/council strategic plans. Grant applications may be acquired from the national office and must be submitted by October 31; those lodges granted awards will be notified by the following January 31. To be eligible for grant consideration, the lodge must have achieved at least the bronze level of Journey to Excellence performance in the year of their submission and have not received a grant from the Order within the last two years.

Founder's Award. The Founder's Award was created 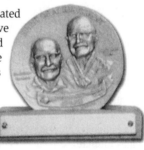 to honor and recognize those Arrowmen who have given outstanding service to the lodge. The award is reserved for those Arrowmen who memorialize in their everyday life, the spirit of achievement as described by founder E. Urner Goodman. The award is a handsome bronze medallion bearing the likenesses of E. Urner Goodman and Carroll A. Edson, and wooden base with a brass plate for engraving. The award is suitable for display at home or the office.
Also available is the Founder's Award arrow ribbon, similar to the universal arrow ribbon, except that it has a gold-colored arrow suspended from a red ribbon.

Lodges may petition the national Order of the Arrow committee to present up to four awards annually, based on lodge membership. If the lodge presents more than one award, at least one must be to a youth under the age of 21.

Red Arrow Award. The award was created in 1967 to recognize individuals who are not members of the Order of the Arrow, for outstanding service to the Order. This attractive award, a red arrow and medallion superimposed on an engraved plaque, and a miniature charm for civilian wear, can be awarded only by action of the national Order of the Arrow committee. Recommendations, by personal letter, must be sent to the director of the Order of the Arrow. The awards are presented at the National Order of the Arrow Conference.

Distinguished Service Award. The Distinguished Service Award was created in 1940 to honor those who render service to the Order beyond the lodge level. The award is presented to those Arrowmen who have rendered distinguished and outstanding service to the Order on a sectional, regional, or national basis. It is given primarily for dedicated service to the Order and Scouting over a period of years.

The first awards were presented at Camp Twin Echo, Pennsylvania, to E. Urner Goodman, Carroll A. Edson, and eight others at the 1940 national meeting. Between 1940 and the first national conference in 1948, the award was presented at national meetings as deserving individuals were found. Thereafter, the award presentation became a traditional part of the pageantry and ceremony of the national conference.

Since the time of the first awards in 1940, 908 Distinguished Service Awards have been presented. This alone is a testament to its high standard of excellence. The award is a sterling silver arrowhead, bearing an arrow pointing upward and to the wearer's right, suspended from a white neck-ribbon upon which are embroidered red arrows. A white square knot embroidered upon red cloth is available for uniform wear, and a miniature silver arrowhead lapel pin is available for civilian wear.

Presentation of the award is limited. Arrowmen whose service records are the most outstanding and extend farthest beyond others in the lodge are usually selected. Nominations are open to both youth and adult Arrowmen. Nominations must be made on form No. 24-201.

Innovation Award. The Innovation Award recognizes chapters and lodges for their efforts in improving the OA program and provides a means to chronicle the best ideas in addition to promoting and sharing them nationwide as "best practices." It recognizes innovation at every level of the organization, and as such, any idea that has been proven to positively impact the chapter, lodge, district, council, or Scouting will be considered.

To be eligible, the lodge must have achieved at least the bronze level of Journey to Excellence performance; and the award petition must be completed and forwarded with the lodge's charter renewal application. Selections will be made by the national Order of the Arrow committee. Two awards will be presented in each region each year. The awards consist of a certificate and a donation of $1,000 to the recipient council's permanently restricted endowment fund.

Unit of Excellence Award. The Unit of Excellence Award identifies those units, and leaders within them, that excel at incorporating the OA into their annual planning. This annual award recognizes units that invite the lodge to conduct quality unit elections, participate in lodge events and meetings, and operate a complete troop/team representative program.

Units that qualify are recognized by the council's lodge with a ribbon for display on the unit flagpole. The Scoutmaster/Coach is recognized with a certificate. The troop/team representative and adviser receive a national recognition patch. They are also entitled to wear a special position patch, available through Supply Group.

Other awards. A variety of recognition items are available from the BSA Supply Group for use by lodges and chapters. These include plaques suitable for engraving, statuettes, and certificates. These may be obtained through your local council service center. While it is not necessary to obtain approval of the national Order of the Arrow committee for these local recognitions, lodges and chapters must have the Scout executive's approval prior to presentation. It is recommended that awards of this type be kept to a minimum so that they are more meaningful to the recipients.

Honorary memberships. The national Order of the Arrow committee does not authorize any form of honorary membership in the Order. There is only one kind of membership—that of registered members of the Boy Scouts of America who have been duly elected to membership in the Order of the Arrow.

The only recognition for nonmembers who are considered worthy of recognition for service to the lodge is through awarding a piece of official Order of the Arrow jewelry, official plaque, statuette, or certificate. These are available from the BSA Supply Group. Approval by the Scout executive is still required prior to presentation. Visiting Scouts or leaders cannot be given honorary memberships in the Order.

The Mission of the Order of the Arrow

The mission of the Order of the Arrow is to fulfill its purpose as an integral part of the Boy Scouts of America through positive youth leadership under the guidance of selected capable adults.

INTERPRETATION AND EXPLANATION

A mission statement is a brief sentence that defines an organization's core objective, its essence. It answers the question, "Why do we exist?" using clear, concise words.

The OA's mission statement is a declaration of our key beliefs and intentions as a Brotherhood. It affirms: a commitment to achieve our purpose, our position within the BSA, and the youth-led, adult-supported partnership that is the hallmark of the Order's success.

Every member should become familiar with the Order of the Arrow's mission statement.

. . . mission . . .

The dictionary defines *mission* as "a sending out or being sent out with authority to perform a special service; an errand." As Arrowmen, we are familiar with this concept. The legend, described by Meteu in the Ordeal ceremony, explains how Chingachgook and Uncas traveled to neighboring villages to warn their nation of an impending "dire and dreadful danger." Their trip was a *mission.*

Note that the definition of mission includes the word "authority." A mission is sanctioned and approved. The Order of the Arrow's authority comes from the organization we serve, the Boy Scouts of America.

. . . an integral part of the Boy Scouts of America . . .

Integral (pronounced ĭn•tĕg'•rəl) means "necessary for completeness, essential, whole, complete, made up of parts forming a whole." The word is used to point out that the Order is an essential, integrated program within the broader Scouting program, not a separate entity.

. . . through positive youth leadership . . .

The word *positive* is an adjective which means "making a definite contribution; constructive" to further describe the leadership qualities expected of Arrowmen. Leadership is about action, about directing, guiding and supporting others. As a result, *positive youth leadership* implies "constructive action" by young people.

Like Scouting itself, the Order is designed to benefit youth. Through *youth leadership*, members under the age of 21 learn by doing, planning and conducting OA program at the chapter, lodge, section, region and national levels. The officers and youth committee chairmen lead meetings, run activities and manage OA finances. Only those members under age 21 may hold office or vote.

. . . under the guidance of selected capable adults.

Adults in the Order serve in advisory capacities. Typically, adults serve as advisers to each youth position. An adviser's role often includes training, counseling, coaching and mentoring youth. Not every adult can be chosen to be an OA adviser. Those appointed usually have noteworthy competencies and an ability to relate well with people, especially young people.

The concept of youth-led, adult-supported partnerships took root during the very first days of the Order. Working with their advisers, young members inducted into the Brotherhood in the first ceremonies, in the summer of 1915, began accepting leadership roles that fall: forming committees to maintain membership records, drafting lodge rules and reworking ceremonies.

With each passing decade, the Order's commitment to youth-led, adult-supported partnerships has grown and evolved. Today, that partnership is more prominent and stronger than ever.

THE PURPOSE OF THE ORDER OF THE ARROW

As Scouting's National Honor Society, our purpose is to:

- *Recognize those who best exemplify the Scout Oath and Law in their daily lives and through that recognition cause others to conduct themselves in a way that warrants similar recognition.*

- *Promote camping, responsible outdoor adventure, and environmental stewardship as essential components of every Scout's experience, in the unit, year-round, and in summer camp.*

- *Develop leaders with the willingness, character, spirit and ability to advance the activities of their units, our Brotherhood, Scouting, and ultimately our nation.*

- *Crystallize the Scout habit of helpfulness into a life purpose of leadership in cheerful service to others.*

INTERPRETATION AND EXPLANATION

The Order of the Arrow's four-part purpose explains our intentions and goals. Each member is expected to understand and be able to explain what the OA is all about. The following paragraphs amplify and expand on the above purpose statement.

As Scouting's National Honor Society, our purpose is to . . .

As *Scouting's National Honor Society*, the Order of the Arrow is in some ways similar to high school national honor societies that recognize outstanding students based on scholarship, leadership, service and character. Selection to membership in the OA is unique, however, because it is controlled by nonmember peers rather than members.

. . . Recognize those who best exemplify the Scout Oath and Law in their daily lives and through that recognition cause others to conduct themselves in a way that warrants similar recognition . . .

This first component of the Order of the Arrow's purpose has been an important concept from the beginning of the Order. It relates directly to the BSA's mission to "prepare young people to make ethical and moral choices over their lifetimes by instilling in them the values of the Scout Oath and Law." By recognizing those Scouts who strive to live their lives according to the Scout Oath and Law with membership (and an OA sash, distinctive pocket flap, membership card and handbook), the OA hopes to motivate other Scouts to act in ways that cause them to be selected for OA membership as well.

. . . Promote camping, responsible outdoor adventure, and environmental stewardship as essential components of every Scout's experience, in the unit, year-round, and in summer camp . . .

Camping is one of the primary methods used in Scouting to help young men grow to maturity; to build self-confidence and a sense of responsibility; and develop qualities of trustworthiness and teamwork. It is in the outdoors that young men learn most about the natural world and the responsibility to care for it; stretch themselves mentally and physically against outdoor challenges; and learn to lead, work cooperatively and care for others in a setting that is both healthy and demanding. Confidence in one's skills and abilities comes through testing, and Scouting provides ample opportunities for that testing—from unit camps to summer camps, from camporees to jamborees, and from local outings to nationally sponsored high-adventure programs. An Arrowman understands that his first responsibility is to his unit, and to helping ensure that the outdoor components of his unit's program are strong.

Synonyms for *promote* include "improve" and "develop," so the OA's involvement is more than the promotion of weekend and summer camp to units—much more. The OA is involved in Scouting's camping and high-adventure programming at many levels.

The word *responsible* conveys our commitment to health and safety, and safe practices in all aspects of our outdoor programs and activities.

Environmental has to do with one's surroundings, conditions and circumstances, including all those that influence life on earth. *Stewardship* relates to one's moral responsibility for the care or administration of a group's resources. *Environmental stewardship* then, is about one's moral responsibility to care for one's surroundings. The OA's love of nature is well documented in its ceremonies and traditions. Our Order's responsibility as stewards of the earth's resources is a logical extension of that love, whether local or national in scope.

> . . . *Develop leaders with the willingness, character, spirit, and ability to advance the activities of their units, our Brotherhood, Scouting, and ultimately our nation* . . .

A direct benefit of OA membership is its ability to impart leadership skills to members and provide opportunities to apply and practice those skills. This is accomplished in a myriad of ways, including formal training at many levels and through the example of experienced leaders themselves. The most important methodology is through the careful and focused coaching and mentoring of youth leaders by talented and committed adult advisers. From the chapter to the lodge, section, region and national levels, the OA places young men in leadership roles and allows them to lead and to learn from their mistakes. Successful advisers mentor young OA leaders to succeed, improving their leadership abilities while carrying out assignments for the OA, Scouting or their community.

Inclusion of the word *willing*, along with the words *character, spirit,* and *ability* as descriptors of leadership, is a direct, though subtle, reference to the line in *The Legend:* "And in every village some were found who were quite willing to spend themselves in others' service." One's spirit has a great deal to do with one's will. Taken together, commitment (*willingness/spirit*), *character* (moral constitution), and competence (skill/*ability*) represent the essence of leadership.

To *advance* means "move forward" or "improve." This section of the purpose refers to an Arrowman's first responsibility—his unit—as well as to the Order of the Arrow itself, The Brotherhood of Cheerful Service, Wimachtendienk, Wingolauchsik, Witahemui, and the Boy Scouts of America, to whom an Arrowman's service is directed.

> . . . *Crystallize the Scout habit of helpfulness into a life purpose of leadership in cheerful service to others.*

This statement has been a part of the OA's purpose from the beginning. Learning and living Scouting's values are of little worth unless those values become a part of the personality and fiber of our members. When Arrowmen strive to live lives of Brotherhood, Cheerfulness, and Service, every day in every way, they are more likely to lead meaningful and fulfilling lives and more likely to contribute to the betterment of our society.

Charity, helpfulness, and principled living are significant, timeless traits identified and nurtured by our country's founding fathers, sustained during our nation's expansion westward, tempered by great national and world conflicts, invigorated by industrial and technological revolutions, and honed by social movements. They remain a significant and important part of our national fabric and the American people to this day.

The Order of the Arrow, as a component of the BSA, recognizes all of this and strives to help ensure its members set the example of citizenship at its finest.

It seemed only natural to base
this honor society
on the legend and traditions
of the Delaware Indians.

American Indian Bibliography

Annual Reports of the Bureau of American Ethnology

Bulletins of the Bureau of American Ethnology

Chippewa and Dakota Indians—*Subject Catalog of Books, Pamphlets, Periodicals, Manuscripts in the Minnesota Historical Society,* St. Paul, 1969

Folk Music: A Catalog of Folk Songs, Ballads, Dances, Instrumental Pieces, and Folk Tales of the United States and Latin America on Phonograph Records, Music Division, Library of Congress, Washington, DC 20540

Freeman, and Smith, *A Guide to Manuscripts Relating to the American Indian,* American Philosophical Society, Philadelphia, 1966

Harding, A. D., and Bolling, *Bibliography of the Articles and Papers on the North American Indians,* Kraus Reprint, N.Y., 1969

Haywood, Charles, *A Bibliography of North American Folklore and Folksong, Volume Two: The American Indians North of Mexico, Including the Eskimos,* 1961

Murdock, George P., *Ethnographic Bibliography of North America,* New Haven, 1960

Official Museum Directory, American Association of Museums, arranged geographically and indexed by topic, 1971

Rouse, I., and Goggin, *An Anthropological Bibliography of the Eastern Seaboard, ESAF Research Publication No. 1,* New Haven, 1947

Ullom, Judith, *Folklore of the American Indians,* Washington, 1969

GENERAL INFORMATION

Boas, Franz, *Primitive Art*, 1962

Brandon, William, *The American Heritage Book of Indians*, illus., 1961

Culin, Stewart, *Games of the North American Indian*, reprint of the Bureau of American Ethnography, 24th annual report, 1907

Curtis, Natalie, *The Indian's Book*, 1968

Denver Art Museum Leaflet Series, 119 pamphlets, about $15 per set

Dockstader, Frederick J., *Indian Art in America*, 1968

Driver, Harold, *Indians of North America*, 1969

Ewers, John C., *Artists of the Old West*, 1965

Feder, Norman, *American Indian Art*, 1971

Johnson, Michael, *Encyclopedia of Native Tribes of North America*, 1999

LaFarge, Oliver, *The American Indian*, 1960

LaFarge, Oliver, *A Pictorial History of the American Indian*, 1956

McCracken, Harold, *George Catlin and the Old Frontier*, 1959

McKenny, Thomas L., and Hall, James, *Indian Tribes of North America: With Biographical Sketches and Anecdotes on the Principle Chiefs*, 1932 repr. 1970

Material Culture Notes, Denver Art Museum, 136 pp.

Miles, Charles, *Indian and Eskimo Artifacts of North America*, 1963

Owen, Roger C., et al., *The North American Indians: A Sourcebook*, 1967

Paterek, Josephine, *Encyclopedia of American Indian Costume*, 1996

Terrell, John U., *American Indian Almanac*, 1971

The Thaw Collection, *Art of the North American Indians*, 2000

PERIODICALS

Akwesasne Notes, Mohawk Nation, P.O. Box 196, Rooseveltown, NY 13683.

American Indian Art Magazine, quarterly, 7045 Third Ave., Scottsdale, AZ 85201

American Indian Quarterly, University of Nebraska Press, 233 N. 8th St., Lincoln, NE 68588

Whispering Wind, P.O. Box 1390, Dept. 3, Folsom, LA 70437

KEY TO ABBREVIATIONS
USED IN "GEOGRAPHICAL INFORMATION"

AA	*American Anthropologist, new series*
AMGLS	*American Museum of Natural History Guide Leaflet Series*
APAM	*Anthropological Papers of the American Museum of Natural History*
ARBAE	*Annual Report of the Bureau of American Ethnology*

ARSI   *Annual Report of the Smithsonian Institute*
BBAE   *Bulletin of the Bureau of American Ethnology*
BPMCM   *Bulletin of the Public Museum of the City of Milwaukee*
CMAI   *Contributions from the Museum of the American Indian,* Heye
            Foundation
INM   *Indian Notes and Monographs,* Museum of the American Indian,
            Heye Foundation
OCMA   *Occasional Contributions from the Museum of Anthropology of the
            University of Michigan*
PAAS   Proceedings of the American Antiquarian Society
PMA   *Papers of the Michigan Academy of Science, Arts and Letters*

GEOGRAPHICAL INFORMATION

Southeast

Bartram, William, *William Bartram on the Southeastern Indians,* 1995

Brannon, D. G., "The Dress of the Early Indians of Alabama," *Arrow Points,*
    pp. 84–92, 1922

Cushman, H. B., *History of the Choctaw, Chickasaw and Natchez Indians,*
    Greenville, 1899

Finger, John R., *Cherokee Indians: The Eastern Band of the Cherokees in the
    Twentieth Century,* 1992

Foreman, Grant, *The Five Civilized Tribes,* 1971

Fundaburk, Emma L., *Southeastern Indians: Life Portraits,* 1969

Fundaburk, Emma L., *Sun Circles and Human Hands: The Southeastern
    Indians—Art and Industry,* 1957

McReynolds, E. C., *The Seminoles,* 1967

Swanton, John R., "Indian Tribes of the Lower Mississippi Valley and Adjacent
    Coast of the Gulf of Mexico," *BBAE,* XLIII, 1911, repr. 1970

Swanton, John R., "Indians of the Southeastern United States," *BBAE,*
    CXXXVII, 1945, repr. 1970

Tiger, Buffalo, and Harry Kersey Jr., *A Life in the Everglades,* 2002

Usner, Daniel H. Jr., *American Indians in the Lower Mississippi Valley,* 1998

Northeast

DeForest, J. W., *History of the Indians of Connecticut,* repr. 1970

Harrington, M. R., *The Indians of New Jersey: Dickon Among the Lenape,* 1963

Hartman, Sheryl, *Indian Clothing of the Great Lakes: 1740–1840*

Lyford, Carrie, *Iroquois Crafts,* 97 pp., 1994

Lyford, Carrie, *Ojibwa Crafts,* 1953

Rainey, F. G., "A Composition of Historical Data Contributing to the Ethnography of Connecticut and Southern New England Indians," *Bulletin of the Archaeological Society of Connecticut*, Ill, 1–89, 1936

Speck, Frank G., "Notes on the Material Culture of the Huron," *AA*, n.s., XIII, 208–28, 1911

Willoughby, Charles C., "Dress and Ornaments of the New England Indians," *AA*, n.s., VII, 499–508, 1905

Willoughby, Charles C., "Houses and Gardens of the New England Indians," *AA*, n.s., X, 423–34, 1908

Plains

Blish, Helen, *Pictographic History of the Oglala Sioux*, 1967

Catlin, George, *Letters and Notes on the North American Indians*

Ewers, John C., *Blackfeet Crafts*, 66 pp.

Grinnell, George B., *The Cheyenne Indians: . . .* , 2 vols., 1923

Lowie, Robert H., *Indians of the Plains*, 258 pp.

Powers, William K. *Indians of the Northern Plains*, 1969

Wissler, Clark, *North American Indians of the Plains*, 1941

California

Heizer, Robert, *Languages, Territories and Names of California Indian Tribes*, 1966

Heizer, Robert, and Whipple, M. A., *The California Indians*, 1951

Kroeber, A. L., "Handbook of the Indians of California," *BBAE*, LXXVIII, 1–995, 1925, repr. 1970

Underhill, Ruth, *Indians of Southern California*, 73 pp.

Underhill, Ruth, *The Northern Paiute Indians of California and Nevada*, 71 pp.

Midwest

Haga, W. T., *The Sac and Fox Indians*, 1958

Hyde, George, *Indians of the Woodlands*, 1962

Kubiac, William, *Great Lakes Indians: A Pictorial Guide*, 1970

Kinietz, W. V., "Indian Tribes of the Western Great Lakes," *OCMA*, X, 161–225, 1940

Radin, Paul, "The Winnebago Tribe," *ARBAE*, XXXVII, 35–550, 1916

Ritzenthaler, R. E., "The Potawatoni Indians of Wisconsin," *BPMCM*, XIX, 99–174, 1953

Ritzenthaler, R. E., *Woodland Indians of the Western Great Lakes*

Skinner, Alanson, "Material Culture of the Menomini," *INM*, n.s., XX, 1–478, 1921

Southwest

Denver Art Museum Leaflet Series—most of these are on the Southwest

Kluckholn, Clyde, et al., *Navaho Material Culture*, 1971

Sides, Dorothy S., *Decorative Art of the Southwestern Indians*, 1961

Swanton, John R., *Indian Tribes of the American Southwest*, 1952

Tanner, Clara Lee, *Southwest Indian Craft Arts*, 1968

Waters, Frank, *The Book of the Hopi*, 1963

Young, Robert W., *The Navajo Yearbook*, 1961

Northwest

Davis, R. T., *Native Arts of the Pacific Northwest*, 1949

Drucker, Philip, *Cultures of the North Pacific Coast*, 1955

Drucker, Philip, *Indians of the Northwest Coast*, 1955

Hawthorne, Audrey, *Art of the Kwakiutl Indians; and Other Northwest Coast Tribes*, 1967

Holm, Bill, *Northwest Coast Indian Art*, 1970

Invararity, R. B., *Art of the Northwest Coast Indians*, 1967

INDIAN ATTIRE

Carr, L., "Dress and Ornaments of Certain American Indians," *PAAS*, n.s., XI, pp. 381–454, 1897

Evans, C. Scott, *The Northern Traditional Dancer*, 1990

Evans, C. Scott, and J. Rex Reddick, *The Modern Fancy Dancer*, 1998

Hungry Wolf, Adolf, *Powwow Dancer and Craftworkers Handbook*, 1999

Kinietz, Vernon, "Notes on the Roached Headdress of Animal Hair Among the North American Indians," *PMA*, XXVI, pp. 463–67, 1940

Koch, Ronald P., *Dress Clothing of the Plains Indians*, 1990

Krieger, H. W., "American Indian Costumes in the United States Museum," *ARSI*, pp. 623–61, 1928

Rush, Beverly, and Lassie Wittman, *Complete Book of Seminole Patchwork*, 1994

Wissler, Clark, "Costumes of the Plains Indians," *APAM*, XVII, pp. 39–91

Wissler, Clark, "Indian Costumes of the United States," *AMGLS*, LXIII, pp. 1–32, 1926

CRAFTS

Austin, Robert J., *A Manual of Fingerweaving,* 2000

Dean, David, *Beading in the Native American Tradition,* 2002

Ewers, John C., *Blackfeet Crafts,* 66 pp., 1945

Ewers, John C., "Crow Indian Beadwork," *CMAI,* XVI, 1959

Hunt, William Ben, *Complete Book of Indian Crafts and Lore,* 1958
(To be used for techniques only; newer and more accurate designs and styles are available.)

Hunt, William Ben, and Burshears, J. F., *American Indian Beadwork,* 1951

Lyford, Carrie, *Iroquois Crafts,* 97 pp., 1943

Lyford, Carrie, *Quill and Beadwork of the Western Sioux,* 116 pp., 1962

Mason, Bernard S., *Book of Indian Crafts and Costumes,* 1946

Miller, Preston, *A Manual of Beading Techniques,* 1971

Orchard, W. C., "Beads and Beadwork of the American Indian," *CMAI,* XI, pp. 3–140, 1929

Orchard, W. C., *Native American Beadwork,* 2002

Speck, Frank G., "Notes on the Functional Basis of Decoration and the Feather Techniques of the Oglala Sioux," *INM,* V, pp. 1–41, 1928

Wissler, Clark, "Indian Beadwork," *AMGLS,* V, pp. 1–32, 1946

Videos (available from most American Indian craft suppliers)

"How to Bead Native American Style"

"How to Make a Native American Dance Shawl"

"How to Make Moccasins"

"Making a Porky Roach"

INDIAN DANCES

Mason, Bernard S., *Dances and Stories of the American Indians,* 1944

Powers, William, *Here Is Your Hobby: Indian Dancing and Costumes,* 1966

Squires, John L., and McLean, Robert E., *American Indian Dances: Steps, Rhythms, Costumes and Interpretations,* 1963

Videos (available from most American Indian craft suppliers)

"Fancy Dance, Vol. 1"

"How to Dance Native American Style"

"Into the Circle"

"Jingle Dress"

"Native American Men's and Women's Dance Styles"

"Powwow Time, Vol. 1"

"Within the Circle"

Lenni Lenape Word List

A

Able, One Who Is Able — Wunita

Abode, Residence — Achpineen

Accomplished One — Pakantschiechen

Active One — Wischixin

Advantage, One Who Gives Advantage Unto Others — Ichauweleman

Adviser — Witatschimolsin

Afoot, He Who Goes Afoot — Pommissin

Aged One — Kikey

Agreeable One — Nachgundin

Agrees, He Who Agrees — Nguttitehen

Aids, One Who Aids — Witawematpanni

Alder Tree — Topi

Alone, One Who Is Alone — Nechoha

Along the Bank — Japeechen

Amusing One — Klakaptonaganall

Ant — Elikus

Ardent One — Segachtek

Arrow — Alluns

Assistant — Witawematpanni

Assists, One Who Assists — Witschindin

Assures, One Who Assures — Kittaptonen

Attention, One Who Gets Attention — Papenauwelendam

Authority, One Who Has Authority — Tschitanessoagan

Away, He Who Goes Away — Elemussit

B

Babbler, One Who Is a Babbler — Wewingtonheet

Bachelor — Kikape

Back, One Who Comes Back — Apatschin

Badger — Gawi

Bald Eagle — Woapalanne

Bald-Headed One — Moschakantpeu

Bear — Machque

Bearded One — Tuney

Beaver — Ktemaque

Bee — Amoe

Behaves, He Who Behaves Well — Wulilissin

Believer — Olsittam

Beloved — Ahotasu

Best — Wulit

Beyond, He Who Looks Beyond — Wulowachtauwoapin

Big — Amangi

Big, One Who Is Big and Wide — Elgigunkhaki

Birch Tree — Wihhinachk

Bird — Awehhelleu

Bird, Blackbird — Tskennak

Bird, Redbird — Mehokquiman

Black — Sukeu

Black Fish — Sukamek

Black Fox	Wulalowe
Black Snake	Sukachgook
Blameless One	Kschiechelensin
Blamelessly, He Who Lives Blamelessly	Wawulauchsin
Blanket	Akquiwan
Bleed, One Who Bleeds Fast	Kschiechgochgihillen
Blessed One	Welapensit
Blue	Schiwapew
Bluebird	Tschimalus
Boat	Amochol
Book	Bambil
Book Reader	Achgindamen
Boulder	Ganschapuchk
Bow (as in bow and arrow)	Hattape
Boy	Skahenso
Boy, Big Boy	Pilapeu
Boy, Little Boy	Pilawetit
Bright	Wachejeu
Broad	Achgameu
Brother	Nimat
Brother, Elder Brother	Chans
Brother, Younger Brother	Chesimus
Brotherhood	Wimachtendienk
Brown	Wipungweu
Buck (deer)	Ajapeu
Buffalo	Sisilija
Builder	Wikhetschik
Bull Frog	Andhanni
Bullfrog	Oleleu
Bushy, a Bush	Achewen
Business Manager	Nanatschitaquik
Busy One	Wischiki
Buys, One Who Buys	Ajummen
Buzzard, Turkey Buzzard	Amatschipuis

C

Calm-Minded One	Klamhattenamin
Camper	Mechmauwikenk
Canoe, Little Canoe	Amocholes
Capable One	Tschitanissowagan
Captain	Lachxowilenno
Carefree One	Ksinelendam
Careful One	Nechasin
Cares, One Who Cares	Anatschiton
Carpenter	Gendatehundin
Cat, Wildcat	Nianque
Cattle Owner	Wdallemunsit
Cautious One	Anatschihuwewagan
Cedar, Red Cedar Tree	Mehokhokus
Cedar, White Cedar Tree	Talala
Certain, One Who Is Certain	Awelendam
Cheerful	Wingolauchsik
Chestnut Tree	Woapiminschi
Chief	Sakima
Chief, Head Chief	Gegeyjumhet
Chief, Mighty Chief	Allowat Sakima
Child	Amemens
Chipmunk	Anicus
Chosen, One	Gegekhuntschik
Clean One	Kschiechek
Clothing	Ehachquink
Cloud	Achgumhok
Clown	Gebtschaat
Cold One	Taquatschin
Collector	Mawachpo

Comes Back, He Who Comes Back	Apatschin	Delights, One Who Delights	Winginamen
Comforts, One Who Comforts	Wulilaweman	Delivers, One Who Delivers	Nihillasohen
Companion	Nitis	Desires, One Who Desires	Gattamen
Comrade	Tschutti	Determined One	Gischitehen
Concerned, He Who Is Concerned	Lachauweleman	Different One	Tschetschpi
		Diligent One	Lilchpin
Confidence, One Who Has Confidence	Nageuchsowagan	Discerning One	Natenummen
		Doctor	Kikehuwet
Contented One	Tepelendam	Dog	Allum
Cook	Sachgachtoon	Dog, Little Dog	Allumes
Cordial One	Wdehiwi	Door	Esquande
Counselor	Atschimolsin	Doorkeeper	Nutschisquandawet
Counsels, One Who Holds Council	Witatschimolsin	Doubtful One	Quilawelensin
		Dove	Amimi
Crane	Taleka	Dove, Wild Dove	Mowichleu
Creates, One Who Creates With Hands	Gischihan	Dreamer	Lungwamen
		Dresses Well, One Who Dresses Well	Wulenensin
Creates, One Who Creates With Mind	Gischeleman	Drum Beater	Pohonasin
Cricket	Zelozelos		

E

Cries, One Who Cries Aloud	Ganschiechsin
Crow	Ahas
Cures, One Who Cures	Kikehuwet
Current, Strong Current	Kschippehellen
Cutter of Wood	Manachewagan

Eagle, Bald Eagle	Woapalanne
Earnest One	Kittlelendamwagan
Easily, One Who Thinks Easily	Apuelendam
East Wind	Achpateuny
Easy One	Ksinelendam
Eater	Mizin
Eight	Chaasch
Elder	Kikeyjumhet
Elder Brother	Chans
Elected One	Gegekhuntschik
Elk	Mos
Elm Tree	Achgikbi
Encourages, One Who Encourages	Gihim

D

Dancer	Gentgeen
Day	Gischquik
Deep Water	Chitquen
Deer	Achtu
Deer, Young Deer	Mamalis

Endurance, He Who Has Endurance	Ahowoapewi
Endures, He Who Endures Pain	Mamchachwelendam
Enjoyable One	Apensuwi
Enjoys, One Who Enjoys	Apendamen
Enlightens, One Who Enlightens	Gischachsummen
Established, One Who Is Established	Tschitanigachen
Esteemed One	Ahoatam
Esteemed, One Who Is Highly Esteemed	Allowelendam
Excellent One	Wdallowelemuwi
Excited One	Glakelendam
Exerts, One Who Exerts Himself	Wischixin
Exhorts, One Who Exhorts	Guntschitagen
Experienced One	Lippoe
Extravagant One	Klakelendam

F

Farmer	Hakihet
Farsighted One	Wulowachtauwoapin
Fast One	Tschitanek
Father, One Who Is a Father	Wetochwink
Few Times	Keechen
Fifth	Palenachtchegit
Fighter	Machtagen
Fine One	Awullsu
Firefly, Lightning Bug	Sasappis
Fire Maker	Tindeuchen
Fireman	Atenkpatton
Firm One	Tschitanigachen

First	Netami
First Aid, He Who Gives First Aid	Achibis
Fish	Names
Fish, Large Fish	Amangamek
Fisherman	Wendamen
Five	Palenach
Flies, One Who Flies	Wschimuin
Fog, Mist	Awonn
Follower	Nosogamen
Forceful One	Achtschinkhalan
Foremost One	Niganit
Forgetful One	Wannessin
Foundation	Epigachint
Four	Newo
Fourth	Neweleneyit
Fox, Black Fox	Wulalowe
Fox, Gray Fox	Woakus
Free One, to Be One's Own Person	Nihillatchi
Friend	Elangomat
Friendly Looking One	Langomuwinaxin
Friendly One	Tgauchsin
Frog	Tsquall
Funny One	Gelackelendam

G

Gardener	Menhakehhamat
Generous One	Wilawilihan
Gentle One	Wulamehelleu
Giddy One	Gagiwanantpehellan
Gives, One Who Gives Back	Guttgennemen
Good, He Who Does Good for Others	Wulihan
Good One	Awullsu

Good-Looking One	Wulinaxin
Good-Natured One	Tgauchsin
Goose, Wild Goose	Kaak
Gracious One	Eluwilissit
Grandfather	Muchomes
Grasshopper	Kigischgotum
Grateful One	Genamuwi
Gray	Wipunxit
Gray Hair	Woaphokquawon
Gray-Headed One	Wapantpeu lenno
Great	Macheu
Great One	Amangi
Great River	Kittan
Great Sea	Kittahikan
Green	Asgask
Groundhog	Gawi
Grows, One Who Grows Fast	Lachpikin
Guard	Nutiket
Guide	Kichkinet

H

Hair, Gray Hair	Woaphokquawon
Handsome One	Wulisso
Half	Pachsiwi
Happy, He Who Makes Others Happy	Lauchsoheen
Happy One	Wulamallessin
Hat, Cap	Allquepi
Hawk	Meechgalanne
Hawk, Fish Hawk	Nimenees
Hawk, Night Hawk	Pischk
Hears, One Who Hears Well	Achginchen

Heart	Wdee
Helpful One	Witscheman
Helper	Witschindin
Hiker	Achpamsin
Hoarse, One Who Is Hoarse	Bihilewen
Honest One	Schachachgapewi
Honorable One	Wulapeju
Honored One	Machelemuxit
Hopeful One	Nageuchsin
Horse	Nenajunges
Horseback Rider	Nenajungeshammen
How, One Who Knows How	Wunita
Humble One	Gettemagelensit
Humility, One Who Has Humility	Tangitehewagan
Hungry One	Gattopuin
Hunter	Elauwit

I

Impatient One	Asgalendam
Indian Language, One Who Speaks	Helleniechsin
Indifferent One	Ajanhelendam
Inquiring One	Natoochton
Instructs, One Who Instructs	Allohakasin
Interpreter	Anhoktonhen

J

Jocular One	Achgiguwen
Journey, One Who Prepares for a Great Journey	Nimawanachen
Joyful One	Wulelendam
Jumps, One Who Jumps	Laktschehellan
Just One	Wulapeju

K

Kind One	Wulilisseu
King, Great King	Kittakima
Kinsman	Langoma
Knife	Kschikan
Knowledge, One Who Has Knowledge	Weuchsowagan
Knows, One Who Knows How	Wunita

L

Lamp	Nendawagan
Lamp Carrier	Nendawen
Large One	Amangi
Laughing One	Gilkissin
Leader	Takachsin
Lean	Alloku
Leisure, One Who Is at Leisure	Ksinachpin
Left-Handed One	Menantschiwon
Life, One Who Gives Life	Lehellechemhaluwet
Lifesaver	Gachpallan
Lifts, One Who Lifts Up	Aspenummen
Listener	Glistam
Little One	Tatchen
Lively One	Achgiguwen
Lives Long, One Who Lives Long	Segauchsin
Lizard	Gegachxis
Load, One Who Carries a Load	Najundam
Long One	Amiga
Looks, One Who Looks Fine	Wulinaxin
Loving One	Ahoaltuwi
Loyal One	Leke
Lucky One	Welapensit

M

Makes, He Who Makes	Gischihan
Man	Lenno
Man, Little Man	Lennotit
Man, Old Man	Mihillusis
Mediator	Etschihillat
Medicine Man	Meteu
Merchant	Memhallamund
Merciful One	Achgettemagelo
Merry One	Wulelendam
Messenger	Elogamgussit
Mighty and Powerful One	Ehalluchsit
Mighty One	Allouchsit
Mild One	Tgauchsu
Mind, One of Calm Mind	Klamhattenamin
Minded, High-Minded One	Machelensin
Minister	Pichpemmetonhet
Mocking, Jesting	Achgiiki
Modest One	Tachpachiwi
Mountain	Wachtschu
Mouse	Achpoques
Mud, Clay	Assisku
Muscle, Clam	Ehes
Muskrat	Damaskus

N

Near	Gattati
Necessary	Acheweli
Neighbor	Pechotschigalit
Nephew	Longachsiss
Night Hawk	Pischk
Nimble One	Wischixin
Nine	Peschgonk
Noisy One	Achgiguwen

| North | Lowaneu |
| Nurse | Nechnutschinget |

O

Oak, Black Oak	Wisachgak
Oak, White Oak	Wipunquoak
Obedient One	Awullsittamuwi
Old One	Kikeyin
Old Tree	Quetajaku
One	Mawat
Opossum	Woapink
Otter	Gunammochk
Overseer	Genachgihat
Owl	Gokhos
Owl, Little Owl	Gokhotit

P

Paddle, Oar	Tschimakan
Pale One	Woaptigihilleu
Panther	Quenischquney
Parent	Wenitschanit
Part, One Who Takes Part	Apendelluxowagan
Partridge	Popokus
Patient One	Papesu
Pays, One Who Pays	Eenhen
Peaceable One	Achwangundowi
Peaceful One	Langundowi
Perplexed One	Ksukquamallsin
Persevering One	Tschitanitehen
Persuades, One Who Persuades	Achtschinkhalan
Physician	Kikehuwet
Pigeon	Amemi
Pine Tree	Kuwe
Pious One	Welilissit

Plenty, One Who Has Plenty	Wiaxowagan
Poplar Tree	Amocholhe
Power, He Who Has Spiritual Power	Mantowagan
Powerful, Most Powerful One	Eluwak
Powerful One	Allohak
Praised, One Who Is Praised	Wulakenimgussin
Praises, He Who Praises	Amentschinsin
Preacher	Pichpemmetonhet
Prepared, He Who Is Prepared	Gischenaxin
Pretty One	Awullsu
Promise, He Who Keeps a Promise	Wulamoen
Proud One	Wulelensin
Prudent One	Wewoatamowi
Puppy	Allumes

Q

| Quick One | Allapijeyjuwagan |
| Quiet One | Klamachpin |

R

Rabbit	Moskimus
Raccoon	Espan
Rattlesnake	Wischalowe
Reader	Achkindiken
Ready, One Who Is Ready	Gischhatteu
Recommended, One Who Is Recommended	Wulakenimgussin
Red	Machkeu
Redbird	Mehokquiman
Redheaded One	Meechgalhukquot

Relates, One Who Relates	Atschimolehan
Reliable One	Nagatamen
Remembers, He Who Remembers	Meschatamen
Restless One	Alachimoagan
Rests, He Who Rests	Alachimuin
Returns, He Who Returns	Apatschin
Rich Man	Pawallessin
Righteous One	Schachachgapewi
River	Sipo
River, One Who Is Along the River, Bank, or Shore	Japeechen
Robin	Tschisgokus
Rock	Achsin
Rock, Big Rock	Ganschapuchk
Runner, Fast Runner	Kschamehhellan

S

Sacrifices, One Who Sacrifices	Wihungen
Saddle	Happachpoon
Sad One	Sakquelendam
Sailor, or Seafarer	Pehachpamhangik
Satisfied One	Gispuin
Satisfies, One Who Satisfies Others	Eenhawachtin
Searches, One Who Searches	Lattoniken
Second	Nischeneyit
Secretary	Lekhiket
Seeker	Elachtoniket
Sees, He Who Sees	Nemen
Sensitive One	Amandamuwi
Sermon	Elittonhink

Servant of the Lord	Allogagan Nehellatank
Serves, He Who Serves	Allogagan
Service	Witahemui
Seven	Nischasch
Sheep	Memekis
Shepherd	Nutemekiset
Silent One	Tschitgussin
Single One	Ngutteleneyachgat
Sings, One Who Sings	Nachgohuman
Six	Guttasch
Skillful One	Wowoatam
Small One	Tangetto
Snake	Achgook
Snow	Guhn
Son	Quis
Sorrowful One	Uschuwelendam
Speaker, Fast Speaker	Lachpiechsin
Speaker, Loud Speaker	Amangiechsin
Speaks, He Who Speaks Favorably	Wulaptonen
Speaks, He Who Speaks Truly	Wulamoc
Speaks, One Who Advocates Our Cause	Wulaptonaelchukquonk
Speaks Plainly, One Who Speaks Plainly (or Pronounces Well)	Wuliechsin
Spirits, He Who Has Good Spirits	Wulantowagan
Spiritual One	Achewon
Spiritual, One Who Has Spiritual Power	Mantowagan
Spruce Tree	Schind
Square One	Haschawije

Squirrel, Flying Squirrel	Blaknik
Squirrel, Ground Squirrel	Anicus
Squirrel, Red Squirrel	Kuwewanik
Star	Allanque
Steady One	Clamhattenmoagan
Stone	Achsin
Stony	Achsinnigeu
Stranger	Tschepsit
Strengthens, One Who Strengthens	Tschitanissohen
Strong One	Achewon
Stronger	Tschitani
Stubborn One	Amendchewagan
Sure One	Bischik
Swiftly, He Who Goes Swiftly	Kschihillen
Swimmer	Aschowin

T

Talker	Wewingtonheet
Talker, Fast Talker	Alappiechsin
Tall One	Gunaquot
Teacher	Achgeketum
Ten	Metellen
Thankful One	Genamuwi
There, One Who Is There	Epit
Thin One	Waskeu
Thinker	Litchen
Thinker, Deep Thinker	Achowelendam
Thinks, One Who Thinks Easily	Apuelendam
Third	Nechit
Thoughtful One	Pennauweleman
Three	Nacha

Tired One	Wiquihillau
Toiler	Achowalogen
Torch Carrier	Nendawen
Trader	Memhallamund
Traveler	Memsochet
Traveler, Night Traveler	Nipahwochwen
Travels, He Who Travels Alone	Nechochwen
Treasurer	Mawachpo
Troubled, the Troubled One	Sakquelendamen
True, He Who Is True	Leke
True, He Who Has Proven True	Gischileu
Trusted, One Who Can Be Trusted	Nagatamen
Trusts, One Who Trusts	Nhakeuchsin
Trustworthy One	Nageuchsowagan
Truth, Speaker of the Truth	Ktschillachton
Truthful One	Wulamoewaganit
Turkey	Tschikenum
Turtle	Tulpe
Twin	Gachpees
Two	Nischa

U-V

Upright One	Wulapejuwagan
Useful One	Apensuwi
Unconcerned One	Ajanhelendam
Understanding One	Pendamen
Unlucky One	Pallikteminak
Valor, Man of Valor	Ilau
Valuable One	Wilawi

Violin Player	Achpiquon	Wind, West Wind	Linchen
Visitor	Kiwikaman	Winner	Wsihuwen
		Wise One	Lippoe
		Wise Man	Wowoatammowino

W-Y-Z

Waits, He Who Waits	Pesoop	Witty One	Luppoewagan
Walker	Pemsit	Wolf	Wiechcheu
Walker, Fast Walker	Kschochwen	Wonderful One	Wulelemi
Walks, He Who Walks Alone	Nechochwen	Wonders, One Who Does Great Wonders	Ganschelalogen
Warrior	Netopalis	Wood Gatherer	Natachtu
Wasp	Amoe	Woodcock	Memeu
Watchman	Wewoapisak	Woodcutter	Giskhaquen
Water	Mbi	Woodpecker	Papaches
Water, Clear Water	Kschiechpecat	Work, One Who Does Good Work	Wulalogewagan
Water, Deep Water	Chuppecat	Worker, Hard Worker	Achowalogen
Water, Still Water	Klampeechen	Worthy One	Elgixin
Weasel	Sanquen	Wounded One	Achpequot
Well Behaved	Welauchsit	Writer	Lekhiket
Well, He Who Is Always Well	Wawulamallessin	Yellow	Wisaweu
West	Wundchenneu	Younger Brother	Chesimus
Whippoorwill	Quekolis	Zealous One	Skattek
White	Wapsu		
Wide One	Achgameu		
Willful	Ahoweli		
Willing One	Nuwingi		
Wind, East Wind	Achpateuny		

Index